TECHNOLOGY

TECHN

LARGE HADRON COLLIDER (SEE PAGES 32–33)

OLOGY

CLIVE GIFFORD

SCHOLASTIC discover more™

How to discover more

This book is simple to use and enjoy, but knowing a little bit about how it works will help you discover more about technology. Have a great read!

How the pages work
The book is divided into chapters, such as **Microchips & smart tech**. Each chapter is made up of stand-alone spreads (double pages) that focus on specific topics.

Timeline spreads
Timeline spreads (pages 24–25, 44–45, 68–69, and 92–93) give you the most important dates and events in the history of technological inventions.

Fantastic facts
BIG text gives an amazing fact or quote!

Step-by-step
Look out for picture sequences that show every step in a process.

Fact boxes
Some spreads include a profile box with details about a specific invention.

How robots work [Nuts and bolts]

Robots are machines that perform difficult, repetitive, or dangerous tasks for us. Most robots gather information about their surroundings using cameras and other sensors. They then follow instructions given by an onboard computer or sent by remote control.

PackBot specifications

Made by	iRobot, US
Introduced	2002
Length (minus flippers)	27 in. (68.6 cm)
Width	16 in. (40.6 cm)
Height (arm retracted)	7 in. (17.8 cm)
Weight (minus batteries)	45 lb. (20.4 kg)
Power	2 lithium-ion batteries
Sensors	Accelerometers, compass, GPS, cameras, inclinometer
Top speed	5.8 mph (9.3 kph)

PackBot
A human operator controls this mobile robot from a distance by remote control. PackBot can detect and disarm bombs, handle dangerous chemicals, and even explore damaged nuclear power stations.

PackBot in action
With its surveillance camera, a PackBot peers into a van thought to contain a bomb.

Multipurpose roving robot
As PackBot moves, it communicates with its controller. It can carry out a range of tasks using arm tools, called end effectors.

Surveillance camera
This color camera can magnify up to 312 times.

LED array
Bright light-emitting diode (LED) lamps illuminate the scene viewed by the camera.

Gripper
This gripper is just one of PackBot's range of arm tools.

Extendable arm
Able to lift 30 lb (13.6 kg), the arm can also turn and work around corners.

Controller
A microprocessor in the body coordinates the robot's actions.

90: the number of seconds it takes to get **PackBot** up and running

Other PackBot arm tools

FLASHLIGHT CABLE CUTTER GLASS BREAKER ROUTE CLEARANCE TOOL KIT

Tracks and flippers
Mobile robots with legs or with tanklike tracks are better at crossing rough ground than wheeled machines are. PackBot's tracks and movable flippers enable the robot to overcome obstacles in its path.

The flippers tilt, and their tracks grip the ground.

Rotating flippers haul the robot over the ridge.

The flippers rotate until they face ahead again.

1 Climbing a ridge
When PackBot reaches the top of a ridge or a sharp dip, the flippers tilt down.

2 Over the top
The flippers then move back and underneath the robot, propelling it forward.

3 Straight ahead
Having overcome the obstacle, PackBot trundles off at up to 8.5 feet (2.6 m) per second.

Rotating flippers

Rounded track belts
Tracks enable PackBot to tackle mud, snow, and steep slopes.

Drive camera
This shows the route ahead, and tilts to give a close view of the gripper.

Digital companion book

Shigeru Miyamoto [Video game creator]

Japanese video game designer Shigeru Miyamoto has dreamed up some of the most exciting and successful video games of all time, including Donkey Kong (1981), which was one of the first-ever video games sold for consoles at home. At the time, video games were mostly played on huge machines at arcades. Miyamoto also created the Super Mario Bros. video games, which are the bestselling games in the world. He is also credited with encouraging the development of Nintendo's Wii system.

220 million
Super Mario video games have been sold since 1985

Discover more about video game consoles

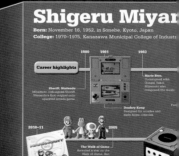

Shigeru Miyar
Born: November 16, 1952, in Sonobe, Kyoto, Japan
College: 1970–1975, Kanazawa Municipal College of Industr

Discover all about the people who created cool technologies.

Click the pop-ups for extra stories.

Spread types

Look out for different kinds of spreads such as stats spreads and photographic spreads. Other spreads explode an amazing technology so you can see everything inside.

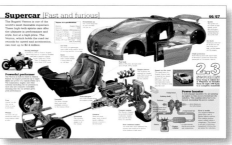

Supercar [Fast and furious]

LOOK-INSIDE SPREAD

A look-inside spread pulls apart a familiar object and explores the different technologies that combine to make it work efficiently.

Net numbers What we do on the Internet.

STATS SPREAD

A stats spread is packed full of facts, amazing statistics, and fun infographics.

PHOTOGRAPHIC SPREAD

This type of spread focuses on an extraordinary subject, often providing an unfamiliar view, such as these thrill seekers on a roller coaster.

More here columns
This feature suggests books to read, places to visit, things to do, and keywords to learn.

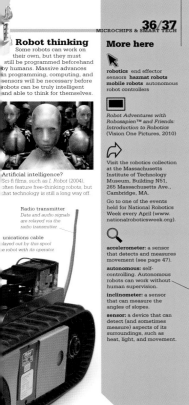

36/37
MICROCHIPS & SMART TECH

Robot thinking

Some robots can work on their own, but they must still be programmed beforehand by humans. Massive advances in programming, computing, and sensors will be necessary before robots can be truly intelligent and able to think for themselves.

Artificial intelligence?
Sci-fi films, such as *I, Robot* (2004), often feature free-thinking robots, but that technology is still a long way off.

Radio transmitter
Data and audio signals are relayed via the radio transmitter.

...unications cable
...played out by this spool
...he robot with its operator.

More here

robotics end effector sensors **hazmat robots** **mobile robots** autonomous robot controllers

Robot Adventures with Robosapien™ and Friends: Introduction to Robotics (Vision One Pictures, 2010)

Visit the robotics collection at the Massachusetts Institute of Technology Museum, Building N51, 265 Massachusetts Ave., Cambridge, MA.

Go to one of the events held for National Robotics Week every April (www.nationalroboticsweek.org).

accelerometer: a sensor that detects and measures movement (see page 47).
autonomous: self-controlling. Autonomous robots can work without human supervision.
inclinometer: a sensor that can measure the angles of slopes.
sensor: a device that can detect (and sometimes measure) aspects of its surroundings, such as heat, light, and movement.

Key to symbols in More here columns

Suggested reading

Keywords for web searches

Fact file

Places to visit

Mini glossary

Watch

Mini-glossary
This explains challenging words and phrases found on the spread.

Glossary and index

The glossary explains words and phrases that might not be explained fully on the spreads or in the **More here** columns. The index can help you find pages throughout the book on which words and topics appear.

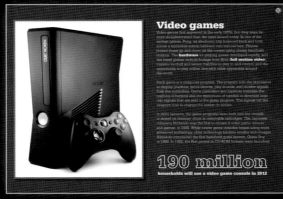

Video games

Video games first appeared in the early 1970s, but they were far more sophisticated than the ones around today. In one of the earliest games, Pong, an electronic blip bounced back and forth across a television screen between two vertical bars. Players moved these up and down on the screen using clunky handheld devices. The **hardware** for playing games developed rapidly, and the latest games include footage from films, **full motion video**, realistic football and tennis matches so play in, and control, and the opportunity to play online, live with other opponents around the world.

Each game is a computer program. The program tells the processors to display graphics, move objects, play sounds, and receive signals from the controllers. Game controllers and joysticks translate the pushing of buttons and the movement of handles or direction keys into signals that are sent to the game program. The signals tell the program how to change the action on-screen.

In older systems, the game programs were built into the console, or stored on memory chips in removable cartridges. The Japanese company Nintendo was the first to release a video game console and games, in 1988. While newer game consoles began using more advanced technology, older technology became smaller and cheaper. Nintendo introduced the first handheld game system, Game Boy, in 1988. In 1992, the first games in CD-ROM formats were launched.

190 million

households will use a video game console in 2012

Read in-depth technology encyclopedia entries.

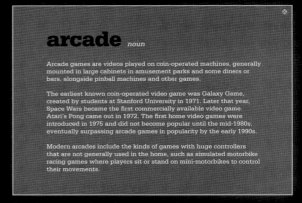

arcade *noun*

Arcade games are videos played on coin-operated machines, generally mounted in large cabinets in amusement parks and some diners or bars, alongside pinball machines and other games.

The earliest known coin-operated video game was Galaxy Game, created by students at Stanford University in 1971. Later that year, Space Wars became the first commercially available video game. Atari's Pong came out in 1972. The first home video games were introduced in 1975 and did not become popular until the mid-1980s, eventually surpassing arcade games in popularity by the early 1990s.

Modern arcades include the kinds of games with huge controllers that are not generally used in the home, such as simulated motorbike racing games where players sit or stand on mini-motorbikes to control their movements.

Look up technology words.

Literacy consultant: Barbara Russ, 21st Century Community Learning Center Director for Winooski (Vermont) School District

Project editor: Steve Setford

Project art editor: Mark Lloyd

Designer: Clare Joyce

US editor: Elizabeth Krych

Art director: Bryn Walls

Managing editor: Miranda Smith

Managing production editor: Stephanie Anderson

Cover designer: Natalie Godwin

DTP: John Goldsmid

Visual content editor: Dwayne Howard

Executive Director of Photography, Scholastic: Steve Diamond

"Any...advanced technology is indistinguishable from magic."
—ARTHUR C. CLARKE, 1961

Library of Congress Cataloging-in-Publication Data Available

ISBN 978-0-545-38373-8

10 9 8 7 6 5 4 3 2 1   12 13 14 15 16

Printed in Singapore   46
First edition, May 2012

Scholastic is constantly working to lessen the environmental impact of our manufacturing processes. To view our industry-leading paper procurement policy, visit www.scholastic.com/paperpolicy.

Contents

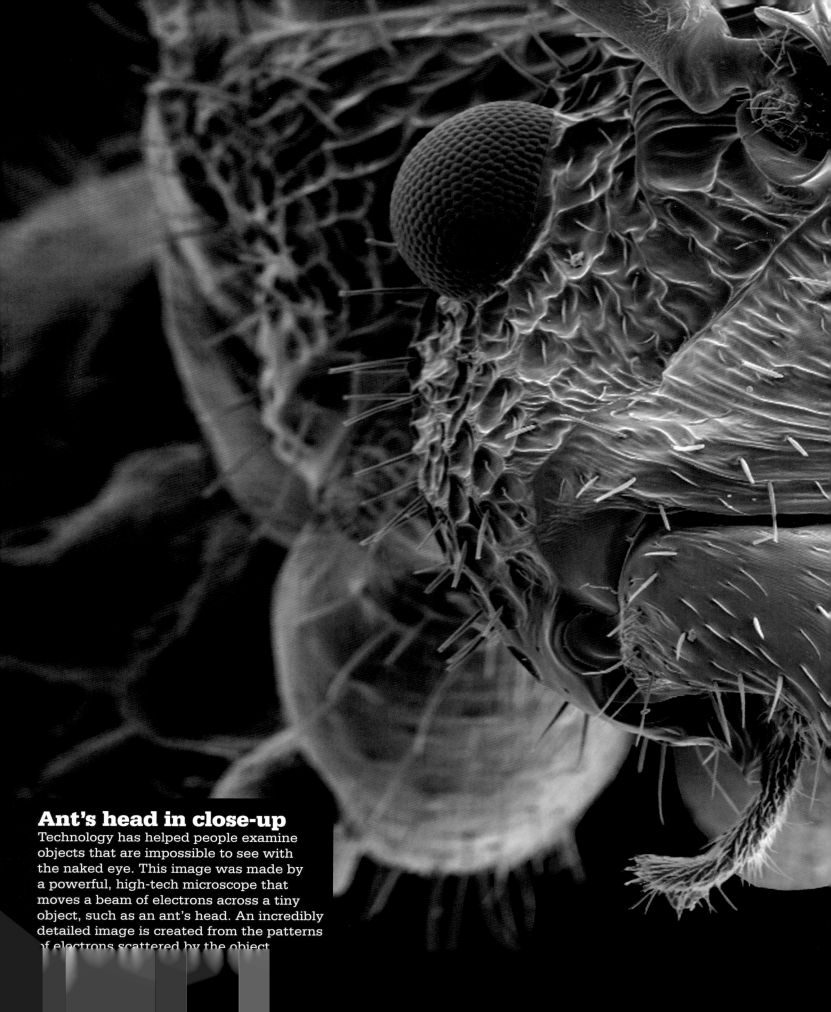

Ant's head in close-up

Technology has helped people examine objects that are impossible to see with the naked eye. This image was made by a powerful, high-tech microscope that moves a beam of electrons across a tiny object, such as an ant's head. An incredibly detailed image is created from the patterns of electrons scattered by the object.

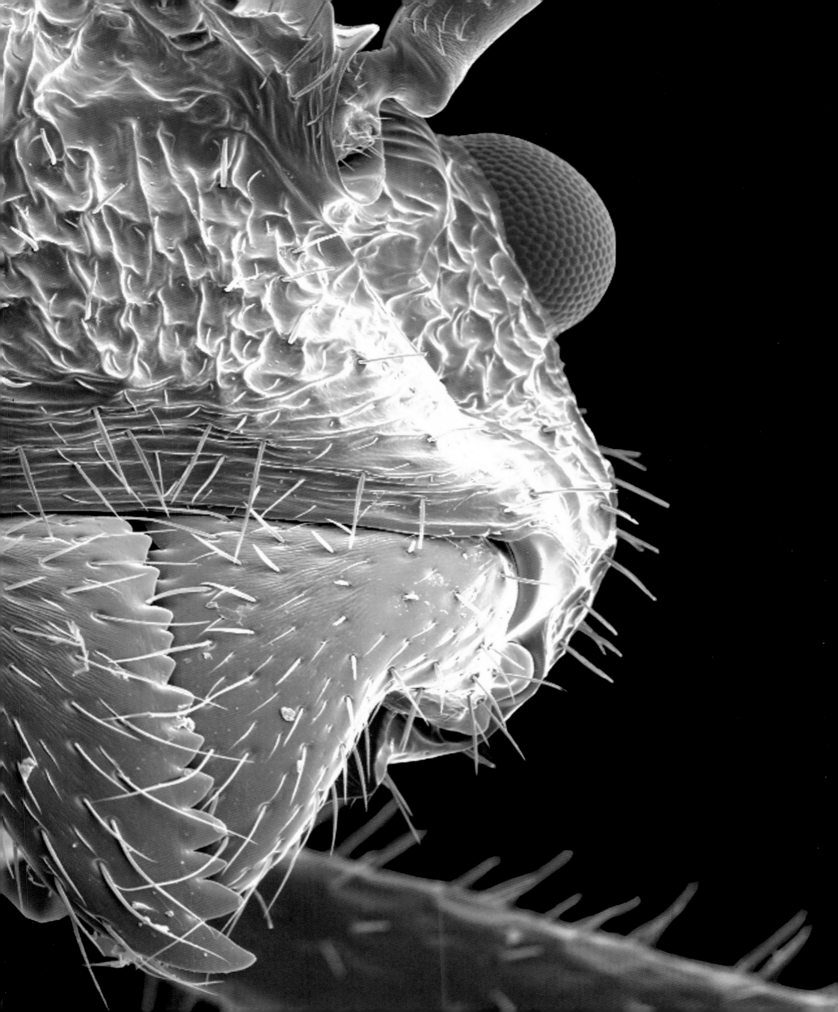

New Mars rover

Curiosity, a robotic vehicle, is tested by scientists in Pasadena, California. In 2012, after traveling 48 million miles (77 million km) through space, Curiosity will look for signs of life on Mars. Since the space program began, scientists have developed technologies to investigate our solar system and the Universe beyond it.

510 LBS

Micro
& sma

* What's so smart about smartphones?

* How can technology help you when you're lost?

* Why do robots play soccer?

chips
t tech

Shrinking tech [Smaller...

In the history of technology, progress sometimes means building bigger and stronger. But many recent advances involve packing more abilities and functions into smaller and smaller spaces.

Phone revolution

Early portable phones resembled walkie-talkies, but they were bulky and heavy. To make them easy to carry, batteries and electronic components had to be shrunk in size.

Pye mobile, 1972
This shoulder-worn device was one of the earliest cell phones. It made calls by dialing into telephone systems.

Car phone, 1982
The Nokia Mobira Senator, the first portable car phone, had its own battery pack so it could be carried around. It weighed a hefty 22 lb. (9.8 kg)!

Martin Cooper
In 1973, a team at Motorola led by Martin Cooper invented the first handheld cell phone. Their prototype was the forerunner of the DynaTAC (see left).

A mobile revolution

The invention of transistors (see next page) helped usher in smaller and more powerful devices such as portable transistor radios and—starting in the 1980s—cell phones. As more and more transistors have been fit onto microchips, cell phones have shrunk in size and grown in power. Today's cells come with many built-in features.

1983

Name	Motorola DynaTAC 8000X
Weight	28 oz. (794 g)
Cool fact	The first handheld cell phone on sale

Expensive pioneer
Standing over 13 in. (33 cm) tall and with a battery that allowed just 30–60 minutes of talk time, the pioneering 8000X cost an astonishing $3,995.

1989

Name	Motorola MicroTAC
Weight	12.3 oz. (349 g)
Cool fact	The first cell phone with a flip-down format

Flip-down first
The MicroTAC was smaller than earlier phones, with a flap that folded down to show its keypad. The screen could display just eight characters.

yet better]

865.7 million:
the number of cell phone users
in India in August 2011

Smaller and smaller

Valves, or vacuum tubes, were used as switches or amplifiers in early radios and computers. They were replaced by small transistors in the 1950s. Microchips began to replace transistors in the 1970s.

TRANSISTOR   MICROCHIP

From valve to microchip
Many millions of transistors can be etched on a single tiny microchip—a fraction of the size of a valve—to provide phenomenal computing power.

VALVE

1996

Name	Motorola StarTAC
Weight	3.1 oz. (88 g)
Cool fact	One of the first phones with lithium-ion batteries

Good vibrations
The smallest, lightest phone at the time, the StarTAC was also the first cell phone that could vibrate as well as ring when it received calls.

2002

Name	BlackBerry 5810
Weight	4.7 oz. (133 g)
Cool fact	The first BlackBerry email/phone device

Surfer's phone
You could email and surf the Internet on the 5810, but since it had no built-in microphone or speaker, you had to attach a headset to make calls.

2011

Name	LG Thrill 4G
Weight	5.93 oz. (168 g)
Cool fact	The first phone with a glasses-free 3-D display

3-D marvel
Two 5-megapixel cameras produce images that merge into a 3-D view on the Thrill's display. It also has Wi-Fi and 8GB of memory.

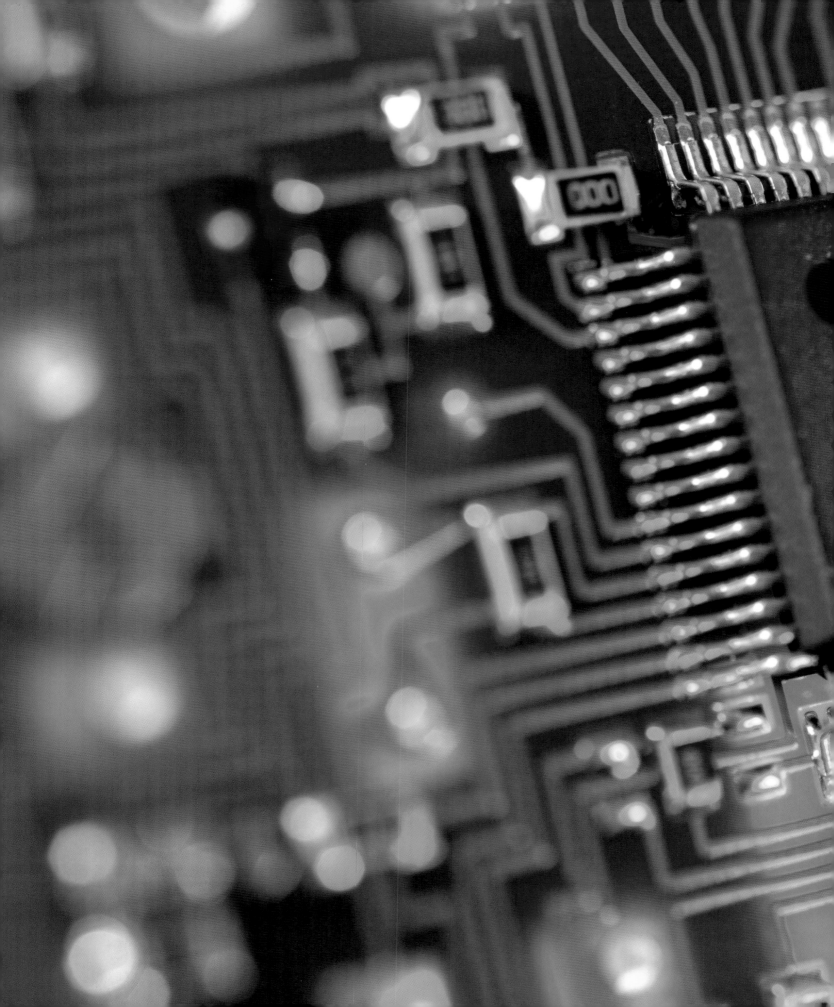

Powerful processor

A computer's microprocessor sits on top of its motherboard—the circuit board that links it to the rest of the computer. The microprocessor, or central processing unit (CPU), is the "brain" that controls most of the computer's functions. It consists of a complex arrangement of transistors (see page 15). Some microprocessors can contain up to 2.6 billion transistors!

Personal computer [Digital

Thousands or millions of transistors (see page 15), working together, enable a personal computer (PC) to perform complex calculations incredibly rapidly. PCs work with digital data—a flow of *1*s or *0*s, each stored as a binary digit (or bit) of memory. This data is represented as an on-or-off flow of electric signals inside a computer's circuits.

Analog and digital

PCs can only use digital data, but much information, such as sound waves, is continuous and varying. This analog data must be sampled and converted into digital data—a series of *1*s and *0*s that represents the original analog information.

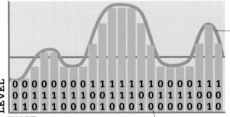

Wavelike analog signal

Converting to digital
An analog-to-digital converter takes small samples of an analog signal and gives a precise number to each sample.

Digital signal
Each digital sample has a precise value in terms of 1s and 0s.

Inside your computer

A PC, like this MacBook Pro i7 laptop, contains many physical components, called hardware. Together with instructions called programs, or software, they enable the computer to store and process digital data. A group of programs called an operating system controls its basic functions.

Airport card
A circuit board and antenna make Bluetooth and Wi-Fi connections.

Superdrive
This can play DVDs and CDs, and record onto blank disks.

RAM chips
Together, these chips provide the computer with 4GB of RAM (see next page).

Hard-disk drive
This drive stores 750GB of data on magnetic disks, which spin up to 7,400 times per minute.

Aluminum unibody
The case is made from a single sheet of aluminum metal that is bent, shaped, and cut.

325
million PCs were sold worldwide in 2010

data device]

Name	Apple I
Introduced	1976
Cool fact	Sold in kit form; 4KB of RAM

Name	Apple MacBook Air
Introduced	2008
Cool fact	Half a million times the memory of the Apple I

PC evolution
Early PCs had no sound or graphics, and limited memory capacity. Data was stored on punched cards or magnetic tape. Modern PCs have many thousands of times more processing power.

Cooling fan
Two fans cool the components to keep them from overheating.

Motherboard
This circuit board holds many of the PC's core components (see right).

The vital parts
The diagram below shows the interaction of the key components involved in handling and storing data and running programs, such as the central processing unit (CPU) and several different types of memory.

Control unit
The CPU's control unit receives and carries out instructions from the memory.

Arithmetic logic unit (ALU)
The ALU, also part of the CPU, performs calculations requested by the control unit.

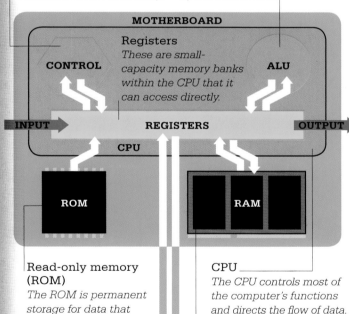

MOTHERBOARD

CONTROL

Registers
These are small-capacity memory banks within the CPU that it can access directly.

ALU

INPUT → REGISTERS → OUTPUT

CPU

ROM

RAM

Read-only memory (ROM)
The ROM is permanent storage for data that does not change or get erased when the PC is switched off. It holds vital instructions, called firmware, that enable the machine to work.

CPU
The CPU controls most of the computer's functions and directs the flow of data.

Random-access memory (RAM)
The CPU uses the RAM to temporarily store data on which it is working.

STORAGE

Rechargeable battery
Making up about 20 percent of the laptop's weight, the battery can power up to seven hours of use.

Storage
A set of memory chips or a hard-disk drive holds programs and the user's personal data.

Smartphone [Power at your

A smartphone is like a small computer in the form of a cellular phone. Able to handle phone calls, texts, and emails, smartphones go way beyond the basics with programs called apps (see page 23), which enable users to perform hundreds of different tasks.

225 million: the number of touches a touch screen is built to take

What's inside?

A smartphone contains a computing system on a microprocessor; memory; and devices to handle its graphics, sounds, and display. A program called an operating system—such as Android, Symbian, or Apple iOS—controls the phone's operation.

Pocket power
A smartphone has more memory and processing power than a personal computer from the 1990s had.

Touch-screen technology

Some smartphones include a small physical keyboard, but most have a touch screen. This displays icons and scroll bars, which users touch or swipe to enter information and commands.

Capacitive layer
Current flowing through this grid creates an electric field across the screen.

Sensing layer
Vertical and horizontal sensor lines detect changes to the electric field.

Glass visual display
Displays are typically 3–4.5 in. (7.6–11.4 cm) across diagonally.

Screen coating
A scratch-resistant coating also reduces reflections, to make the display easier to read in bright light.

3 Disturbed field
The transfer of charge disturbs the electric field on the capacitive layer.

2 Finger touch
When the user touches the screen, charge transfers to the finger.

4 Sensors
The change in the electric field is measured by sensors.

1 Screen charge
A small electric charge is applied to the screen from all four corners.

Capacitive screen
Many touch screens use a capacitive system, which detects changes to an electric field caused by the touch of a finger.

5 Alerting controller
The sensors send data to the screen's controller, which calculates where on the screen the touch occurred.

Exploded phone
A smartphone is packed full of parts, and even its screen consists of several different layers. As many as 2,000 individual components have to fit into its slim casing, which is often made of tough, lightweight plastic.

fingertips]

Removable storage card
A microSD (Secure Digital) card lets the user transfer data and photos to and from computers.

Speaker
Sounds are broadcast to the user's ear.

SIM card
The subscriber identity module (SIM) memory chip stores phone numbers and other personal information.

Digital camera
Photos taken by the user can be stored in the memory and sent to other people.

Microprocessor
A powerful processor is the smartphone's computing center.

Image and video processor chip
This allows the phone to play videos on its display.

Lithium-ion battery
(See box below.)

Lightweight casing

Wi-Fi transmitter and receiver
The phone can access the Internet whenever a Wi-Fi hotspot is nearby.

Microphone
The user's voice is changed into electrical signals.

RAM chip
The operating system is stored on a random-access memory (RAM) chip.

Metal shield
This protects the electronic parts.

Lithium-ion battery

Recharging a phone's flat battery causes all its ions (electrically charged lithium atoms) to move from the positive terminal to the negative terminal. When the phone is used, the ions flow in the opposite direction, from negative to positive.

Negative terminal

Positive terminal

Lithium ions

Electron flow

Electricity supply

Ions move to negative terminal

Ions move to positive terminal

Electron flow

Phone

1 No charge
With all the ions at the positive terminal, the battery is flat and can provide no power.

2 Charging
The ions begin to flow when the phone is plugged into an electricity supply.

3 Fully charged
With all the ions now at the negative terminal, the battery is ready to use again.

4 In use
Electrons power the phone. Lithium ions flow back to the positive terminal.

Making calls | Get connected

Cell phones work by changing speech, text messages, and images into radio waves. The radio waves travel to their destinations via radio antennae called base stations. When you make a call, you set in motion an amazing sequence of events.

Cell phone network

A cellular phone network is divided into thousands of areas called cells, each with a base station. A cell's size depends on the number of calls made in that area. Busy city cells are small, because they each have to handle many callers. Cells work in groups of seven, with each group linked to a ground station.

Phoning a friend

The call starts when you dial your friend's number. As you talk, the phone changes your words into electrical signals.

Transmitter/ receiver

PERSON A

Incoming sound
This is sent by your friend's phone.

Outgoing sound
This is sent by your phone.

1 Sending
A microprocessor inside the phone converts electrical voice signals into digital data. Your phone sends the data as radio waves to a local base station.

Base station

Cell

4 Group to group
Ground stations relay the call between cell groups. Longer-distance calls may be sent via a communications satellite.

Ground station

Your location

3 Cell to cell
If you are on the move, the call is routed from one cell to another and transmitted from the nearest base station.

Mobile Telephone Switching Office

2 Tracking calls
Verification signals are sent to a Mobile Telephone Switching Office (MTSO). The MTSO keeps track of the phone's location.

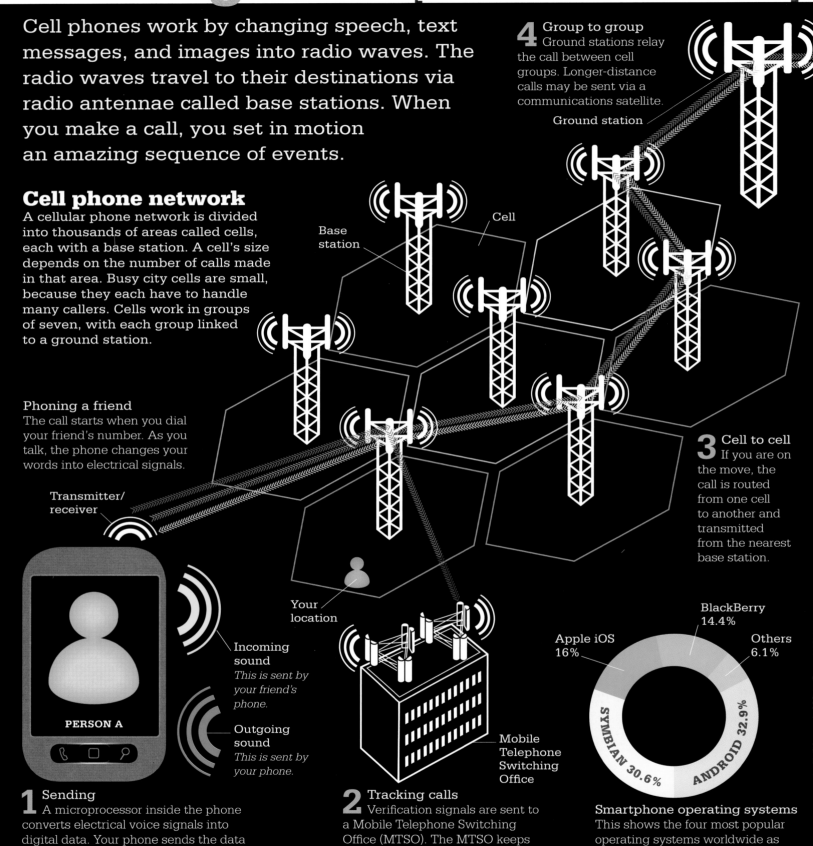

BlackBerry 14.4%

Apple iOS 16%

Others 6.1%

SYMBIAN 30.6%

ANDROID 32.9%

Smartphone operating systems
This shows the four most popular operating systems worldwide as of early 2011 (see page 20).

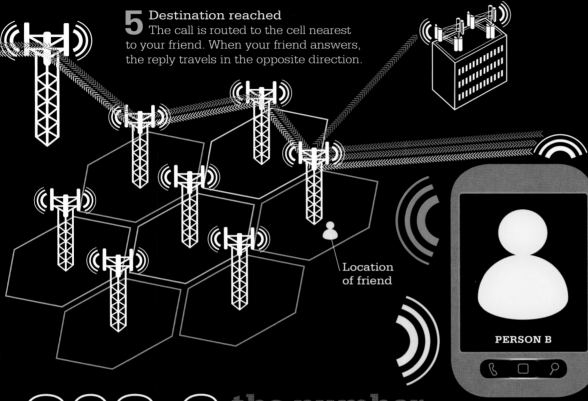

5 Destination reached
The call is routed to the cell nearest to your friend. When your friend answers, the reply travels in the opposite direction.

Location of friend

PERSON B

302.6 million:

the number of smartphones sold worldwide during 2010

6 Receiving
Your friend's phone converts the radio signal back into electrical signals, and a speaker broadcasts your voice.

Applications
Apps can be downloaded from the Internet to a smartphone. These small, efficient computer programs give your smartphone extra capabilities. Apple's online iPhone store contains over 500,000 different apps.

Social networking
Some apps give access to sites such as Facebook, Twitter, and LinkedIn.

Sounds
These apps are for listening to radio stations and music, and making recordings.

Navigation
Some apps use maps and GPS (see pages 30–31) to help you find your way around.

Games
The most popular apps are games, ranging from quizzes and puzzles to action games.

Text
Websites, news feeds, and electronic books can be read on-screen with these apps.

Travel
Travel apps may provide tourist information and up-to-date plane and train travel times, or translate foreign languages.

Types of app
Here are some popular types of app. They do not include utilities—apps that improve your phone's performance.

More here

Profiles: Tech Titans by Carla Killough McClafferty

Read the life stories of the founders of Google, the company that developed the Android operating system for smartphones.

Android iOS **apps** augmented reality **IBM Simon** SMS communications satellite

Dallas Museum of Art, 1717 North Harwood, Dallas, TX

Visit one of the first museums to offer a smartphone tour that adds commentary, facts, and images on visitors' smartphones as they view exhibits.

Mobile Telephone Switching Office (MTSO): a computer system that tracks phone calls and their locations, transfers calls between cells, and tracks the length and cost of calls.

short message service (SMS): a protocol that allows text messages of up to 160 characters to be sent between cell phones.

Information technology

The first computers were unreliable machines used only by specially trained technicians to make complex calculations. In little more than 50 years, computers have developed into powerful tools that anyone can use for work, learning, and entertainment.

1971
Microprocessor
The first general-purpose computer microprocessor (see pages 16–17) was the Intel 4004. It combined many of the key components of a computer onto a tiny wafer of silicon, called a silicon chip or microchip.

INTEL 4004
CHIP CASE

1642
Calculator
PASCAL'S MACHINE

A practical mechanical calculator, the Pascaline, was invented by French mathematician Blaise Pascal when he was only 18. It could add numbers up to eight digits long.

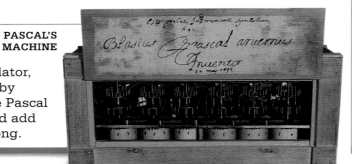

1943
Colossus, the first programmable electronic computer, was used in England to crack German codes during World War II.

Dots represent 10-year increases.

1956
American computer company IBM introduced its 350 Disk Storage Unit— the first hard-disk drive (see page 18).

1971
In the US, the first electronic mail (email) message was sent over a computer network by Ray Tomlinson, a computer programmer.

1974
One of the first computers on sale to the public, the Altair 8080, came as a kit and had to be built by the buyer.

1960•   1970•

1946
The Electronic Numerical Integrator and Computer (ENIAC), developed by the US Army, could do more than 5,000 calculations per second.

1963
At California's Stanford University, Douglas Engelbart and Bill English built the first computer mouse.

1834
Mechanical computer
Englishman Charles Babbage designed his analytical engine, a device that would be able to perform a range of mathematical tasks. He never completed it.

ANALYTICAL ENGINE (INCOMPLETE)

1951
UNIVAC I
Costing $1.5 million, UNIVAC I was the first mass-produced, commercially available computer. UNIVAC I stored information on magnetic tape and punched cards.

12.8 tons: the weight of a UNIVAC computer in the 1950s

[The computer age]

BILL GATES
American pioneer

Founded:	Microsoft Corp.
Developed:	Windows operating system

1985
Microsoft vs. Apple

Microsoft released its Windows operating system (see page 18), which was used on many PCs. Rival company Apple, which launched its first Macintosh (Mac) computer in 1984, used its own operating system.

STEVE JOBS
American pioneer

Founded:	Apple Inc.
Developed:	Apple computers, tablets, and iPods

1991
World Wide Web

The web is a vast collection of electronic pages (web pages) that can be viewed on computers via the Internet (see pages 26–29). Devised in 1989, it was first made available to the public in 1991.

AN ARTIST'S IDEA OF THE WEB

1981
The Epson HX-20—the first laptop-size portable computer—was launched. It was powered by a rechargeable battery.

1997
IBM's Deep Blue computer defeated world chess champion Garry Kasparov, 3½–2½, in a 6-game series.

1990• **2000•** **2010**

1996
Universal Serial Bus (USB) connectors, used to link electronic devices to computers, were introduced.

2004
The Facebook social networking site (see page 29) was started by Mark Zuckerberg and his friends.

2005
The YouTube website was launched. YouTube allows users to share their videos with others online.

2008
Search engine company Google claimed that its database contained at least 1 trillion web pages.

1976
Supercomputer

The Cray-1, the first supercomputer, was built in the United States by Seymour Cray, an electrical engineer. It could make millions of calculations per second but weighed 5.5 tons.

CRAY-1 SUPERCOMPUTER

2010
Apple iPad

The iPad was Apple's first tablet—a handheld computer with a touch screen. In terms of size and weight, tablets are between laptops and cell phones.

APPLE iPAD TABLET

2,507 trillion:
the number of calculations per second that China's Tianhe-1 supercomputer can perform

Internet [Spanning the globe]

The Internet is sometimes called the world's biggest machine. In fact, it is millions of machines—computers, routers, and servers (see below)—all linked together with wired and wireless connections. Common rules, called protocols, enable them to work together so that people can send emails, upload and download files, play games against one another online, and view pages from the World Wide Web.

Information highway

Internet data can travel as electrical signals along phone lines, as radio signals relayed by space satellites, or as pulses of light through very thin glass strands inside fiber-optic cables. Most home computers connect to the Internet via a modem.

Home computer and modem
When you click on a link to a web page on your computer, the modem converts the digital request from your computer into an analog signal. This signal is sent over a phone, coaxial, or fiber cable as packets of data.

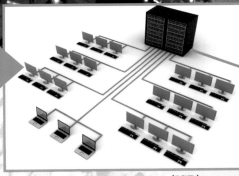

Internet service provider (ISP)
The data packets requesting the web page arrive at the computers of an ISP, a company that manages your Internet connection. Devices called routers direct your request to the correct destination.

Microsoft data center
Owned by Microsoft, this building in Chicago can house up to 224,000 servers that operate 24 hours a day, 7 days a week. In total, data centers consume around 1.3 percent of the world's entire electricity supply.

More here

20 Things I Learned About Browsers and the Web (available for free at www.20thingsilearned .com/en-US)

How Did That Get to My House?: Internet by Gary Chmielewski

computer network
Vinton Cerf **ARPANET**
Tim Berners-Lee
Internet backbone
domain name server

client: in a computer network, a computer or device that requests information.

exabyte: a unit of information or computer storage that is equal to one quintillion bytes.

internet traffic: the amount of data sent via the Internet, often measured by month.

server: a computer that relays data or resources to client computers in a computer network.

Data center
Internet information, such as the web page you want to view, is usually stored at data centers. These are collections of special computers called servers, which receive and respond to requests for information.

Web page
Your home computer has its own unique address, called an IP address. Servers and routers on the Internet use this address to direct the flow of information—in this case, a web page—back to your computer.

80.5:
the number of exabytes of Internet traffic predicted per month for the year 2015 (that's enough to fill 20 billion DVDs)

Net numbers

From its humble origins in the 1970s as a computer network linking universities and other large organizations in the United States, the Internet has mushroomed. Today, more than 2 billion people are online with access to the Internet.

Emailing

Electronic mail (email) involves sending text messages over the Internet. Photos, videos, and music files can also be attached to an email. In 2010, over 107 trillion emails were sent—that's more than 3.4 million every second!

Global email
This is how the world's 2.9 billion email accounts are distributed. About a quarter of these are business accounts.

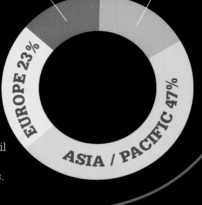

North America 14%

Rest of the world 16%

EUROPE 23%

ASIA / PACIFIC 47%

Surfing

People surfing, or browsing, the World Wide Web (see page 25) can ask search engines to help them find the website or information they want. Google, with over 36,000 requests per second, is the most popular search engine.

Web growth
The number of websites hosted on the World Wide Web has boomed since the web became accessible to the public in 1991.

204
SEPTEMBER 1993

300,000
JULY 1996

255,000,000
JULY 2011

Interlinked world

Through emailing, social networking, gaming, and surfing, the Internet connects people across the globe.

Gaming

Video games can be played online via specialized gaming websites or social networking sites (see opposite page). Some are simple one-player games. Others involve complex graphics, virtual worlds, and thousands or even millions of players competing against one another simultaneously.

55,502,307
active users played the FarmVille game on Facebook in 2011

Socializing

Social networking websites help people keep in touch with their friends—both old and new—and share their interests with others. They include Facebook, LinkedIn, and Twitter. Facebook is the biggest of them all.

KEY

👤 = **2 MILLION PEOPLE**

Top Facebook users
The five countries shown below had the most Facebook members in September 2011.

1 UNITED STATES 155,746,780 — 50% of its population

2 INDONESIA 40,420,180 — 17% of its population

3 INDIA 36,421,720 — 3% of its population

4 TURKEY 30,735,100 — 42% of its population

5 UNITED KINGDOM 30,337,440 — 48% of its population

Shopping

Many companies, such as the online retailer Amazon.com, use websites to sell their products by mail order. Buyers of software, videos, and music can often download products directly to their computers and smartphones.

Online auctions
With more than 6.4 million new items for sale each day, eBay is the largest Internet auction site.

SOLD 2001
$4,900,000 GULFSTREAM II JET
Priciest completed sale on eBay

SOLD 2004
£61,000 50,000-YEAR-OLD MAMMOTH SKELETON
Strangest completed sale on eBay

Blogging

Short for *web log*, a blog is a personal journal on the World Wide Web. Blogs are updated regularly with the opinions and feelings of the author (the "blogger"). Many have photos and links to websites and other blogs.

170 million: **the number of blogs in September 2011**

Navigation [Help from above]

Originally designed for the US military, the Global Positioning System (GPS) is a network of satellites that helps users on Earth find their location, accurate to within a few feet. It is one of several satellite navigation systems worldwide. Russia's system, GLONASS, became available to the public in 2007, while the European Union's Galileo project is expected to be operational by 2018.

Solar panel
Energy from the Sun's rays powers the satellite.

Fin for tagging
A tag is usually fitted to a shark's dorsal fin. After a set amount of time, the tag detaches itself and rises to the surface.

Satellites above

GPS currently relies on 24 satellites. Each satellite orbits Earth twice each day, continually transmitting its precise location. It also transmits the time, which is calculated by onboard atomic clocks to within billionths of a second.

GPS network
Groups of 4 satellites travel on 6 different orbits. From almost any place on Earth, a GPS receiver can obtain signals from at least 4 of the 24 satellites.

Finding your position
The GPS receiver uses the positions of the satellites in space and the time differences in the arrival of their signals to calculate its own location on Earth.

Satellite signals
Signals from the different satellites arrive within milliseconds of one another.

Person with receiver
The receiver uses the signals to find its location.

12,550

miles (20,200 km): the approximate altitude above Earth's surface of each GPS satellite

Great white shark
Large marine animals, such as great whites, are often tracked with pop-up tags, which float to the surface and beam signals to an Argos satellite.

Keeping track

A satellite system called Argos allows researchers to track the movements of wild animals. A small tag attached to an animal gathers and stores data. It then sends the data to one of the Argos satellites, which uses radio waves to relay signals back to the researchers.

Great white journey
A tag fitted to a great white shark nicknamed Nicole allowed researchers to map its 99-day journey from the coast of South Africa to Australia. On its long swim, the shark traveled 6,800 miles (11,000 km)!

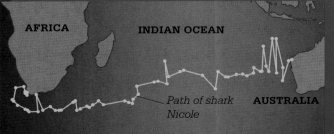

AFRICA
INDIAN OCEAN
AUSTRALIA
Path of shark Nicole

Everyday uses

GPS receivers can be integrated into microprocessors (see pages 16–17) and put inside many electronic devices. For example, voice-guided GPS instruments can give drivers maps and spoken directions to their destinations.

Mapping on the move
A smartphone with a GPS receiver and mapping software can locate the user and show the way to nearby attractions.

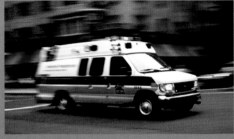

Emergency!
By keeping track of their vehicles with GPS, ambulance services can direct the closest one to the scene of an accident.

At the ends of the Earth
GPS works all over the world. Even polar explorers and scientists can use GPS to navigate in icy, featureless landscapes.

Particle collider [Smashing!]

Deep below the French–Swiss border lies the biggest physics experiment ever. The Large Hadron Collider (LHC) is a long, circular tunnel packed with high-tech gear. Here, scientists smash together tiny particles of matter called protons. They hope to see even smaller particles, never before observed.

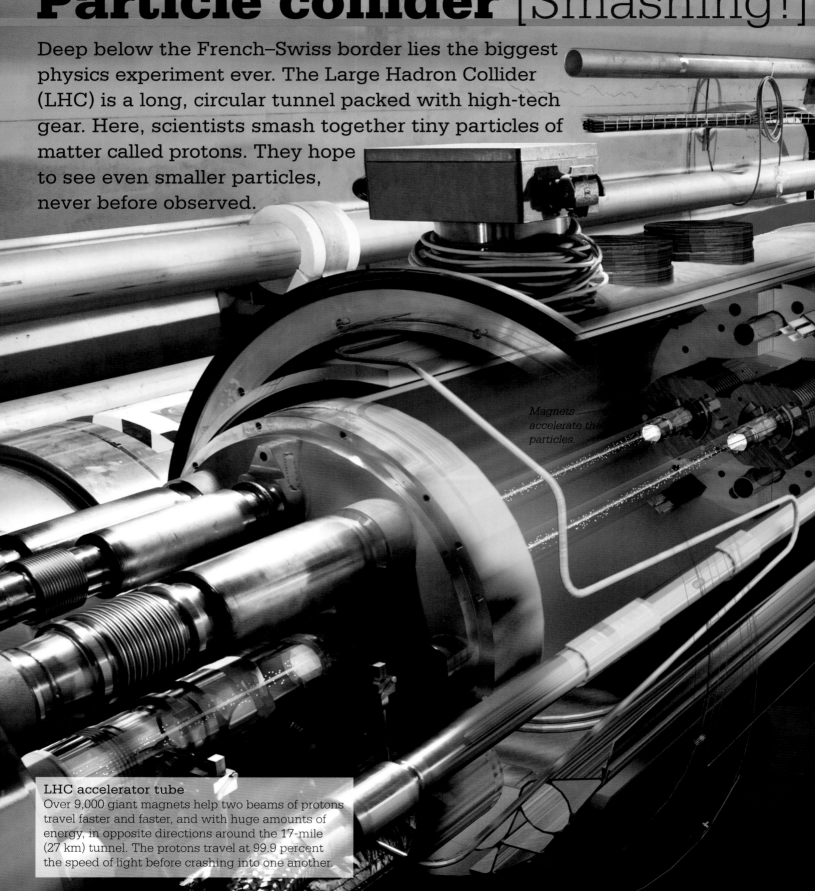

Magnets accelerate the particles.

LHC accelerator tube
Over 9,000 giant magnets help two beams of protons travel faster and faster, and with huge amounts of energy, in opposite directions around the 17-mile (27 km) tunnel. The protons travel at 99.9 percent the speed of light before crashing into one another.

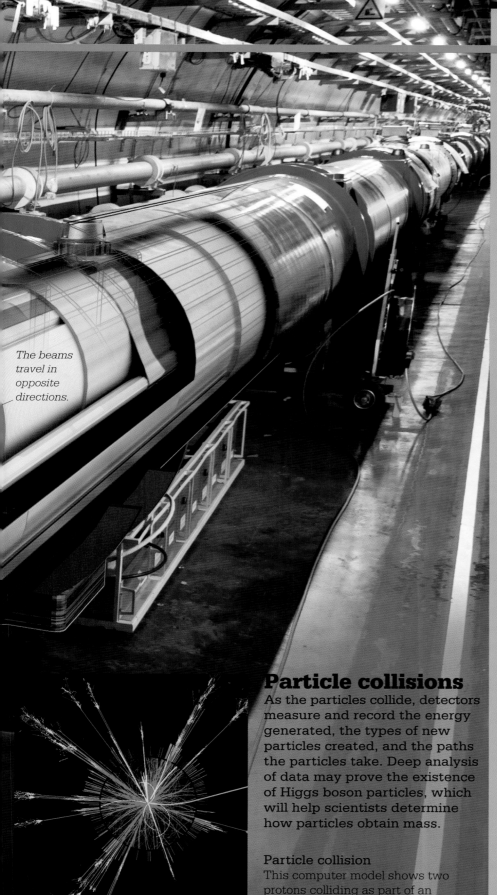

The beams travel in opposite directions.

Seeing the invisible

Human eyes were the most powerful tool for seeing for thousands of years, until the invention of glass lenses. New technologies continue to be developed to help scientists see increasingly smaller and smaller objects.

1021 — The first magnifying glasses allowed people to clearly see the body parts of small creatures, such as insects.

CA. 1590 — The first optical microscopes were invented. Within a century, new microscopes allowed people to see individual plant cells for the first time.

1931 — The first electron microscope, which uses a beam of electrons, was made. Today's scanning electron microscopes (SEMs) can make visible the inner structure of crystals and tiny bacteria.

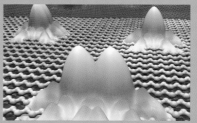

SEM IMAGE OF AN ANT'S EYE

1981 — The scanning tunneling microscope (STM), a type of electron microscope, was developed. STMs can produce images of individual atoms.

STM IMAGE OF MANGANESE ATOMS

2008 — Scientists fired the first protons around the Large Hadron Collider and observed subatomic particles.

Particle collisions

As the particles collide, detectors measure and record the energy generated, the types of new particles created, and the paths the particles take. Deep analysis of data may prove the existence of Higgs boson particles, which will help scientists determine how particles obtain mass.

Particle collision
This computer model shows two protons colliding as part of an experiment at the LHC called ATLAS.

> **"I think we are on the verge of a revolution in our understanding of the Universe. . . . [The] LHC is certainly, by far, the biggest jump into the unknown."**
> —BRIAN COX, BRITISH PHYSICIST AT THE LHC

Spy tech

Spies have always used technology in ingenious ways, both to learn an enemy's secrets and to protect their own from discovery. Many of the most famous spy stories date from the Cold War—the period after World War II when the United States and the Soviet Union were great rivals.

BADGE OF THE KGB, THE SOVIET SECRET SERVICE (1954–1991)

Goldfinger (1964)
In this movie, Bond's Aston Martin DB5 car contained machine guns, a bulletproof screen, and an ejector seat.

Bond . . . James Bond

The most famous fictional spy, James Bond, is always equipped with the latest gear, thanks to tech chief Q and his team of researchers and engineers. Bond's many gadgets have ranged from tracking devices and a jet pack to an exploding pen.

Spy satellites identify objects the size of an orange from 185 miles (300 km) above Earth's surface

Wheel cipher

In the 1790s, Thomas Jefferson (later the third US president) created his own cipher machine. The edge of each of its 26 wheels was randomly marked with the letters of the alphabet. When the wheels were moved to spell out a received sequence of scrambled letters, another row gave the real message.

Code maker
Jefferson used this machine to turn his documents into code.

THOMAS JEFFERSON (1743–1826)

Listening device

A wooden depiction of the United States' Great Seal hung on a wall in the US embassy in Moscow for over six years. It had been presented as a gift by the Soviet Union in 1945, but in 1952, the embassy discovered that the seal contained a bug. It had been relaying conversations to Soviet spies outside the building.

Eavesdropping
The Soviet spies listened to conversations by bouncing radio waves off the bug.

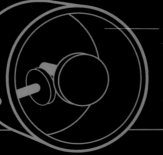

Sound waves made the bug's cover vibrate, which altered the radio waves returning to the spies.

THE BUGGED GREAT SEAL

Minicamera

MINOX film cameras were used by spies of many nations to copy documents. One such agent was John A. Walker Jr., a US Navy officer who spied for almost 20 years for the Soviet KGB before his arrest in 1985. He took so many photos that his camera allegedly wore out.

Miniature marvel
Measuring 3 in. (7.5 cm) long and weighing as little as 4.5 oz. (130 g), a MINOX camera was small enough to hide in the palm of a spy's hand.

JOHN A. WALKER JR., LEFT (B. 1937)

U-2 spy plane

Fast, unarmed spy planes carrying incredibly powerful zoom cameras can fly over enemy territory and monitor what's happening below. In service since 1955, the Lockheed U-2 plane has flown thousands of spy missions for the United States, and a fleet of 32 U-2s will be in service until at least 2015.

Captured pilot
A U-2 pilot, Gary Powers, was captured by the Soviets in 1960. He was released in a 1962 swap with a US-held KGB spy.

GARY POWERS (1929–77)

Memory stick

Spy tech isn't always specially made gadgets—spies often just use ordinary information technology (IT) devices. In 2010, Russian-born Anna Chapman was arrested in New York. The FBI claimed that she and other spies used USB memory sticks, laptops, and Wi-Fi to exchange secret data.

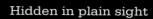

Hidden in plain sight
Computer data can be stored on a memory stick. No one would suspect that it holds vital secrets.

ANNA CHAPMAN (B. 1982)

Online spies

The United States' Cyber Command tries to keep spies from using the Internet to hack into military computer networks to steal data.

Headquarters
Cyber Command operates from this building at the US Army's Fort Meade base in Maryland

1.8 billion
**the number of attacks o:
US government compute
systems every month**

How robots work

Robots are machines that perform difficult, repetitive, or dangerous tasks for us. Most robots gather information about their surroundings using cameras and other sensors. They then follow instructions given by an onboard computer or sent by remote control.

PackBot specifications

Made by	iRobot, US
Introduced	2002
Length (minus flippers)	27 in. (68.6 cm)
Width	16 in. (40.6 cm)
Height (arm retracted)	7 in. (17.8 cm)
Weight (minus batteries)	45 lb. (20.4 kg)
Power	2 lithium-ion batteries
Sensors	Accelerometers, compass, GPS, cameras, inclinometer
Top speed	5.8 mph (9.3 kph)

PackBot

A human operator controls this mobile robot from a distance by remote control. PackBot can detect and disarm bombs, handle dangerous chemicals, and even explore damaged nuclear power stations.

PackBot in action
With its surveillance camera, a PackBot peers into a van thought to contain a bomb.

Multipurpose roving robot
As PackBot moves, it communicates with its controller. It can carry out a range of tasks using arm tools, called end effectors.

Gripper
This gripper is just one of PackBot's range of arm tools.

90: the number of seconds it takes to get PackBot up and running

Other PackBot arm tools

FLASHLIGHT   CABLE CUTTER   GLASS BREAKER   ROUTE CLEARANCE TOOL KIT

Tracks and flippers

Mobile robots with legs or with tanklike tracks are better at crossing rough ground than wheeled machines are. PackBot's tracks and movable flippers enable the robot to overcome obstacles in its path.

Rotating flippers

Rounded track belts
Tracks enable PackBot to tackle mud, snow, and steep slopes.

The flippers tilt, and their tracks grip the ground.

Rotating flippers haul the robot over the ridge.

The flippers rotate until they face ahead again.

1 Climbing a ridge
When PackBot reaches the top of a ridge or a sharp dip, the flippers tilt down.

2 Over the top
The flippers then move back and underneath the robot, propelling it forward.

3 Straight ahead
Having overcome the obstacle, PackBot trundles off at up to 8.5 feet (2.6 m) per second.

bolts]

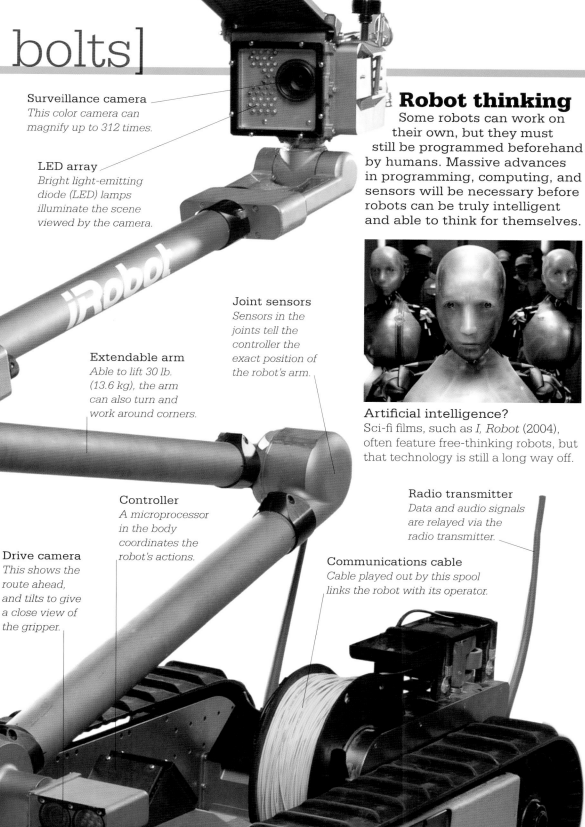

Surveillance camera
This color camera can magnify up to 312 times.

LED array
Bright light-emitting diode (LED) lamps illuminate the scene viewed by the camera.

Joint sensors
Sensors in the joints tell the controller the exact position of the robot's arm.

Extendable arm
Able to lift 30 lb. (13.6 kg), the arm can also turn and work around corners.

Controller
A microprocessor in the body coordinates the robot's actions.

Drive camera
This shows the route ahead, and tilts to give a close view of the gripper.

Radio transmitter
Data and audio signals are relayed via the radio transmitter.

Communications cable
Cable played out by this spool links the robot with its operator.

Robot thinking

Some robots can work on their own, but they must still be programmed beforehand by humans. Massive advances in programming, computing, and sensors will be necessary before robots can be truly intelligent and able to think for themselves.

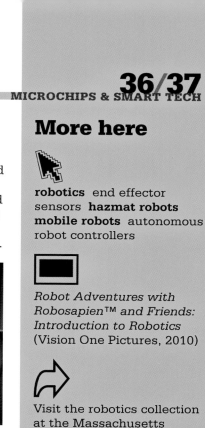

Artificial intelligence?
Sci-fi films, such as *I, Robot* (2004), often feature free-thinking robots, but that technology is still a long way off.

More here

robotics end effector sensors **hazmat robots mobile robots** autonomous robot controllers

Robot Adventures with Robosapien™ and Friends: Introduction to Robotics (Vision One Pictures, 2010)

Visit the robotics collection at the Massachusetts Institute of Technology Museum, Building N51, 265 Massachusetts Ave., Cambridge, MA.

Go to one of the events held for National Robotics Week every April (www. nationalroboticsweek.org).

accelerometer: a sensor that detects and measures movement (see page 47).

autonomous: self-controlling. Autonomous robots can work without human supervision.

inclinometer: a sensor that can measure the angles of slopes.

sensor: a device that can detect (and sometimes measure) aspects of its surroundings, such as heat, light, and movement.

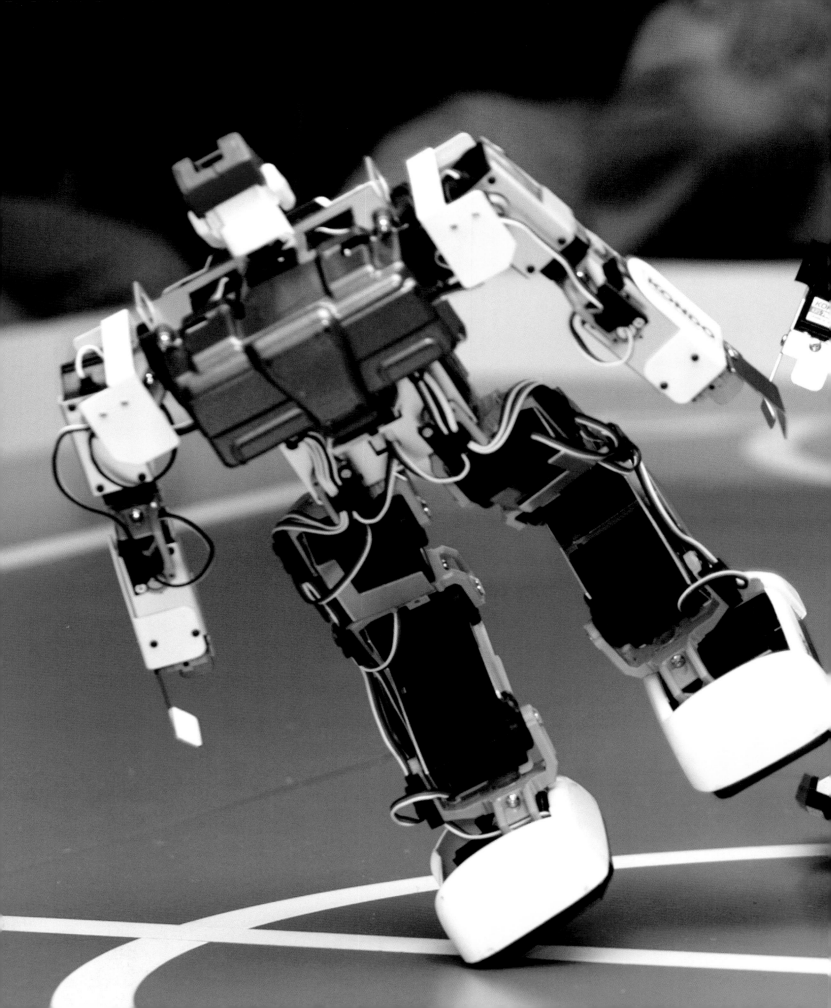

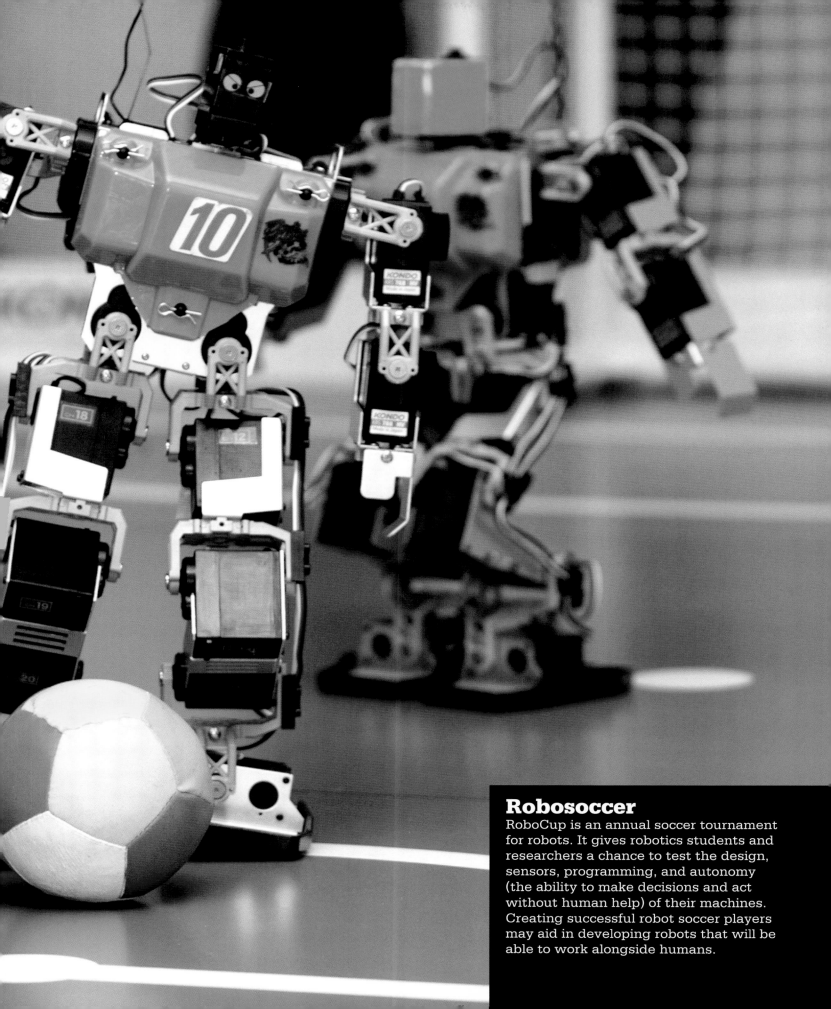

Robosoccer

RoboCup is an annual soccer tournament for robots. It gives robotics students and researchers a chance to test the design, sensors, programming, and autonomy (the ability to make decisions and act without human help) of their machines. Creating successful robot soccer players may aid in developing robots that will be able to work alongside humans.

Robots in action

In 1961, the first industrial robot, Unimate 1, began work at a car factory in the United States. Today, millions of robots are in use worldwide. Robots can work more accurately and for longer than humans, and in conditions too hostile for people to endure.

Fanuc S420i

Able to weld metal parts and also handle heavy loads, the Fanuc S420i has worked in factories for many years. Other industrial robots can spray-paint and handle toxic chemicals.

Welding robot
Sparks fly as a Fanuc S420i welds joints on a car body in an automobile factory.

What does it do?	Welds metal parts together
Built by	Fanuc, Japan
Introduced	1994

Canadarm2

This robotic arm moves astronauts, equipment, and cargo around the International Space Station (see pages 82–83). It travels along rails on the outside of the space station.

What does it do?	Works on the ISS
Built by	Canadian Space Agency
Introduced	2001

Astronaut's assistant
Held by Canadarm2, an astronaut attaches a camera to the ISS.

Da Vinci

Guided by a human surgeon, the Da Vinci robot performs operations in hospitals. It has three arms to wield surgical instruments and one to hold a camera, which relays 3-D images back to the surgeon.

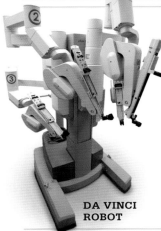

DA VINCI ROBOT

What does it do?	Performs surgery under human control
Built by	Intuitive Surgical, Inc., US
Introduced	1999

More than 8.37 million:
the number of industrial and service robots working worldwide

Autosub3

An autonomous underwater vehicle (AUV), *Autosub3* maps the seabed and makes scientific investigations. It can travel for 250 mi. (400 km) and dive to 5,250 ft. (1,600 m).

What does it do?	Conducts ocean research
Built by	University of Southampton, UK
Introduced	2005

Polar research
Autosub3 can investigate hard-to-reach places, such as under sea ice.

Gostai Jazz

Robot security guards such as the Gostai Jazz patrol homes, offices, and factories. They raise the alarm when their sensors detect intruders, fire, or smoke.

What does it do?	Guards buildings
Built by	Gostai, France
Introduced	2010

Robot on patrol
The Jazz can follow a programmed route around a building, sending video over the Internet to a human manager.

Digital camera
Using face-recognition software and this digital camera, Autom can identify individual human faces and follow a person's movements.

Eye contact
Electric motors move the eyes to point at a person's face.

Autom
This research robot interacts with people every day to help them change their behavior, such as eating more healthily. It can talk to encourage them, using speech software linked to an amplifier and speaker.

What does it do?	Acts as a life coach to humans
Built by	MIT Media Lab, US
Introduced	2007

Fun, g
& th

* Why do 3-D movies and TV shows seem so real?

* Where are the world's scariest roller coasters?

* What makes an electric guitar rock?

ames,
rills

Computer gaming [From

The first chess and tic-tac-toe computer programs were written in the 1950s. But it was the development of microprocessors (see pages 16–17) and personal computers (PCs) in the 1970s that kick-started a gaming revolution.

1977
Atari 2600
This console did not have built-in games. Instead, games had to be loaded from separate cartridges that were plugged into the console.

CLIVE SINCLAIR
British inventor

Founded: Sinclair Research Ltd
Developed: ZX80, ZX81, Spectrum, and QL computers

1980–82
Home computing
The introduction of budget computers, including Sinclair computers in the United Kingdom and Commodores in North America, led to a boom in home computing. Many video games were developed for these low-cost devices.

1989
Creative Labs' first Sound Blaster card for personal computers brought high-quality sound to PC video games.

1951
British company Ferranti made the Nimrod computer specifically to play the mathematics game Nim.

1967
American Ralph Baer invented the gaming joystick. In 1968, he made a video game console, the Brown Box.

1960 •   **1970** •

Dots represent 10-year increases.

1962
The first action game, Spacewar!, was created by programmers in the US.

1977
In the US, Bruce Artwick began work on a flight simulator game (Microsoft's Flight Simulator 1.0 of 1982).

1978
Taito of Japan launched the Space Invaders arcade game, one of the most popular games ever.

1980
Using new graphics techniques, Atari created Battlezone, a three-dimensional (3-D) arcade game.

1972
Pong
This arcade tennis game from US company Atari was the first commercially successful video game. A version for use on home TVs came out in 1975.

PLAYING PONG ON A TV SET, 1977

SHIGERU MIYAMOTO
Japanese designer

Company: Nintendo
Developed: Donkey Kong, Mario, Legend of Zelda

1981
Donkey Kong
Designed by Shigeru Miyamoto, Nintendo's Donkey Kong was one of the first "platform" games. These games require the player to overcome obstacles and jump between suspended platforms.

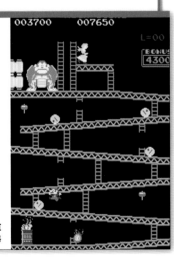

SCENE FROM DONKEY KONG

Pong to Wii]

1998
Dance Dance Revolution
The first commercially successful arcade dancing game, Dance Dance Revolution, was produced by Konami. A version with a plastic dance mat for home gaming consoles went on sale soon after.

ARCADE VERSION OF DANCE DANCE REVOLUTION

75.66 million:
the number of copies of Wii Sports sold by 2011, making it the bestselling computer game ever

2006
Nintendo Wii
This system uses a handheld wireless controller, the Wii Remote, to sense the movements of the gamer (see page 47).

WII CONTROLLER AND CONSOLE

1994
The Hagenuk MT-2000 was the first cellular phone with a built-in game, the falling brick puzzle game Tetris.

2006
The newly released Sony PlayStation 3 (PS3) and Nintendo Wii consoles battled with the Microsoft Xbox 360 (2005) for popularity.

•1990   2000   2010

2000
Electronic Arts published The Sims, which simulated the daily lives of people in a suburban house.

2004
Nintendo released its DS handheld game system, the first with a touch screen and a microphone.

2010
Sony released the PlayStation Move motion-sensing controller for the PS3 console.

2010
Xbox Kinect
Kinect, for Microsoft's Xbox 360, detects motion without the use of a handheld controller (see page 47).

KICKING ACTION WITH KINECT

WAVEBIRD CONTROLLER

2002
Going wireless
The first wireless controller, the WaveBird, was released for Nintendo's GameCube. It sent signals to the console via radio waves.

2005
Guitar Hero
First produced for Sony's PlayStation 2 console, this music game has a guitar-shaped controller.

GUITAR HERO CONTROLLER

Games controller [Sensing

For video games to work well, players need fast, responsive controllers to send commands back to the console. Many devices now use motion sensing, in which the whole controller is moved to simulate actions in a game, from thrusting a sword to hitting a ball.

Mobile gaming

Many games on smartphones or tablets use the device's touch screen to provide game controls. Others, such as racing games, use accelerometers (see next page) to make cars or characters move.

Angry Birds
Run on operating systems (see page 20) such as Apple iOS, Android, and Symbian, Angry Birds uses touch-screen controls to catapult birds around the screen.

500 million
copies of Rovio's Angry Birds game have been sold since its 2009 release

Joystick
Early joysticks, like the Atari 2600 stick, were gripped with the whole hand. Many modern joysticks are smaller, built into game pads, and controlled by a player's thumb.

ATARI 2600 JOYSTICK, 1977

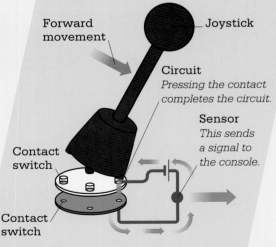

PAC-MAN

Forward movement — Joystick

Circuit
Pressing the contact completes the circuit.

Sensor
This sends a signal to the console.

Contact switch

Contact switch

Switches
Pushing a joystick in one direction closes a switch on its base. This sends a signal indicating whether the joystick was pushed left, right, forward, or backward.

Force feedback
Found in joysticks and game pads, this feature makes the controller wobble or vibrate, giving a sensation of force when a car crashes or a character hits a wall during a game.

NINTENDO 64 CONTROLLER, 1996

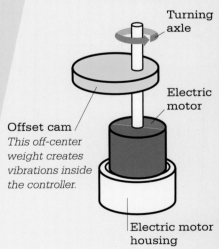

DIDDY KONG RACING

Turning axle

Electric motor

Offset cam
This off-center weight creates vibrations inside the controller.

Electric motor housing

Rumble pack
This pack plugs into a controller. It has a motor that spins an off-center weight and causes the controller to vibrate when the game action gets exciting.

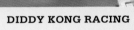

motion]

Motion sensing

Accelerometers (see below) sense changes in the controller's speed and direction of movement, which are converted into on-screen actions.

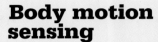

WII REMOTE, NINTENDO, 2006

Body motion sensing

Microsoft's Kinect does not need a physical controller. The player's motions are scanned and tracked by sensors. The console translates this movement into actions within the game.

iCONTROLPAD GAME PAD, 2011

3-D depth sensor

Color camera

3-D depth sensor

KINECT FOR XBOX 360, MICROSOFT, 2010

Mobile controllers

Add-on Bluetooth devices provide gaming controls for smartphones and tablets. The iControlPad unit has direction, movement, option, and fire buttons.

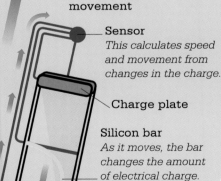

WII SPORTS BASEBALL

DANCE CENTRAL

VELOCISPIDER

Direction of movement

Sensor
This calculates speed and movement from changes in the charge.

Charge plate

Silicon bar
As it moves, the bar changes the amount of electrical charge.

Charge plate

Capacitive accelerometer
Movement bends a silicon bar, altering the charge between two plates. A sensor then calculates the controller's acceleration.

3 Displaying
The player's movements are converted into actions in the game.

1 Sensing
The Kinect IR sensor recognizes a player standing in its depth picture.

2 Tracking
The sensor tracks moving body parts, up to 30 times each second.

Infrared (IR)
A projector sends out IR light, which bounces back to the console. A camera collects the light and builds an image of the room and the player's position.

Smartphone
The phone's Bluetooth chip receives the signals and sends data back to the controller.

Radio signals

Controller
A Bluetooth chip inside sends signals carrying the player's instructions.

Bluetooth
This low-power radio technology allows a games controller and a smartphone, console, or tablet to communicate over distances of up to 33 feet (10 m).

Camcorder [Capturing the

Digital cameras use microchip technology (see pages 15–17) to record images. Still cameras capture a single image, or frame, but camcorders record multiple images one after another, often at a rate of 25 or 30 frames per second. Replayed at the same rate, the individual frames seem to merge to produce a moving picture.

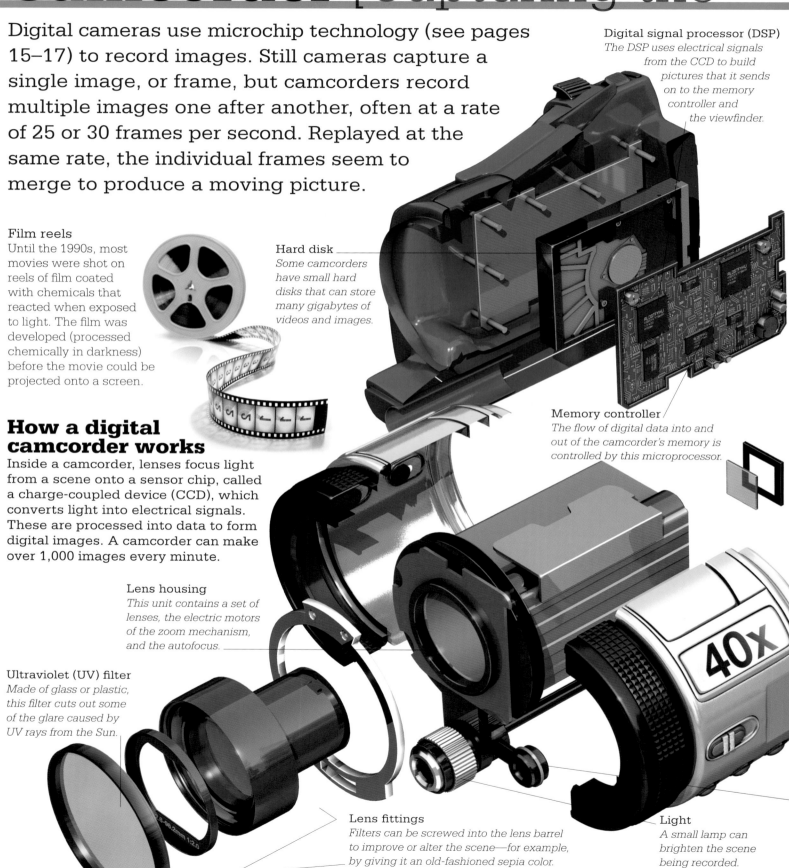

Digital signal processor (DSP)
The DSP uses electrical signals from the CCD to build pictures that it sends on to the memory controller and the viewfinder.

Film reels
Until the 1990s, most movies were shot on reels of film coated with chemicals that reacted when exposed to light. The film was developed (processed chemically in darkness) before the movie could be projected onto a screen.

Hard disk
Some camcorders have small hard disks that can store many gigabytes of videos and images.

How a digital camcorder works
Inside a camcorder, lenses focus light from a scene onto a sensor chip, called a charge-coupled device (CCD), which converts light into electrical signals. These are processed into data to form digital images. A camcorder can make over 1,000 images every minute.

Memory controller
The flow of digital data into and out of the camcorder's memory is controlled by this microprocessor.

Lens housing
This unit contains a set of lenses, the electric motors of the zoom mechanism, and the autofocus.

Ultraviolet (UV) filter
Made of glass or plastic, this filter cuts out some of the glare caused by UV rays from the Sun.

Lens fittings
Filters can be screwed into the lens barrel to improve or alter the scene—for example, by giving it an old-fashioned sepia color.

Light
A small lamp can brighten the scene being recorded.

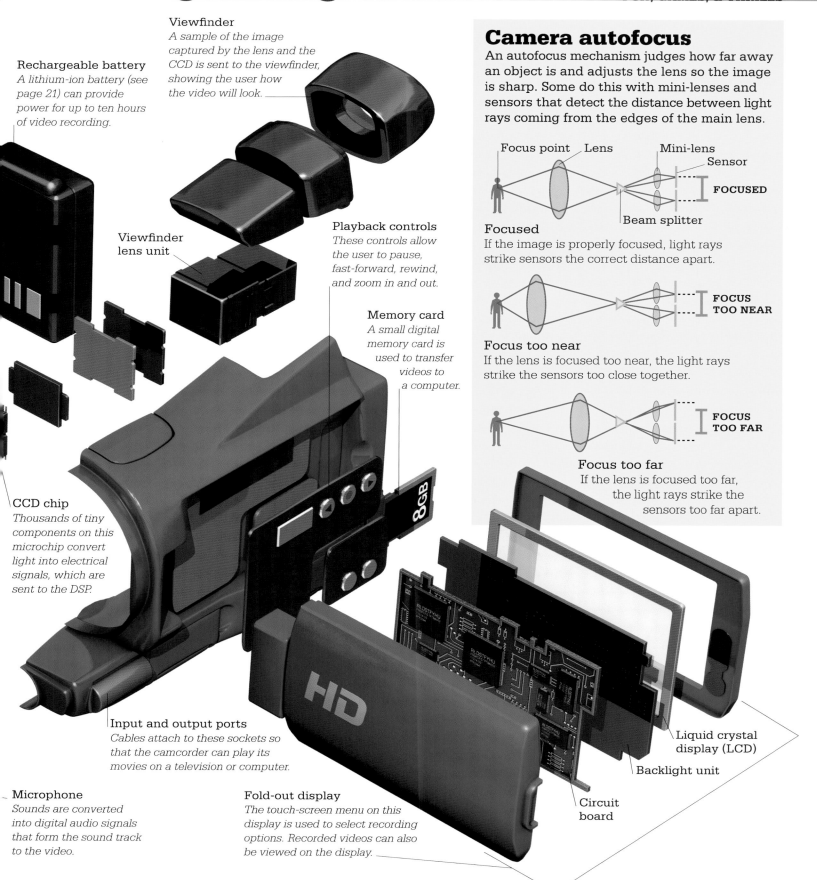

Viewfinder
A sample of the image captured by the lens and the CCD is sent to the viewfinder, showing the user how the video will look.

Rechargeable battery
A lithium-ion battery (see page 21) can provide power for up to ten hours of video recording.

Viewfinder lens unit

Playback controls
These controls allow the user to pause, fast-forward, rewind, and zoom in and out.

Memory card
A small digital memory card is used to transfer videos to a computer.

CCD chip
Thousands of tiny components on this microchip convert light into electrical signals, which are sent to the DSP.

8GB

Input and output ports
Cables attach to these sockets so that the camcorder can play its movies on a television or computer.

HD

Microphone
Sounds are converted into digital audio signals that form the sound track to the video.

Fold-out display
The touch-screen menu on this display is used to select recording options. Recorded videos can also be viewed on the display.

Circuit board

Liquid crystal display (LCD)

Backlight unit

Camera autofocus

An autofocus mechanism judges how far away an object is and adjusts the lens so the image is sharp. Some do this with mini-lenses and sensors that detect the distance between light rays coming from the edges of the main lens.

Focus point   Lens   Mini-lens
                          Sensor
                          FOCUSED
Beam splitter

Focused
If the image is properly focused, light rays strike sensors the correct distance apart.

FOCUS TOO NEAR

Focus too near
If the lens is focused too near, the light rays strike the sensors too close together.

FOCUS TOO FAR

Focus too far
If the lens is focused too far, the light rays strike the sensors too far apart.

When you watch something in 3-D, this optical technology tricks your brain into viewing images the same way as you see everyday life. TV, movie, and game creators use special digital cameras and screens to create 3-D effects. With 3-D glasses, the illusion of depth puts you in the middle of the action.

Natural 3-D

Your eyes view scenes in two dimensions (2-D). To see the world in 3-D—with objects appearing at different distances—your brain processes the image that each eye sees and uses the slight differences between them to build a 3-D scene.

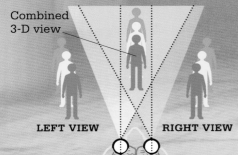

Combined 3-D view

LEFT VIEW   RIGHT VIEW

Optic nerves connect to the brain.

Stereopsis

Each eye sees the same scene from a slightly different angle. Your brain puts the two views together to create a 3-D image. This process is known as stereopsis.

3-D technology

A 3-D movie or TV show is filmed with several cameras that capture slightly different views of the same scene. A special viewing device, screen, or pair of glasses then directs each of the separate images to a different eye.

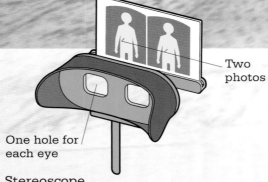

Two photos

One hole for each eye

Stereoscope

This early 3-D device uses two 2-D images of a scene taken from slightly different viewpoints. Each eye views one image through the stereoscope. The brain merges the two images into a single 3-D picture.

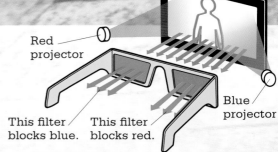

Red projector

This filter blocks blue.   This filter blocks red.

Blue projector

Red and blue

Many 3-D TV and movie systems project two views of the scene in different colors. 3-D glasses have a different colored filter in each lens. The filters let certain colors through to each eye.

Wearing stereoscopic glasses, people can wander through a complete 3-D scene.

Caveman
The Cave Automatic Virtual Environment (CAVE) at Teesside University, UK, uses a series of projectors to display 3-D images on three walls and the floor of a specially built room.

This filter blocks vertical rays.

This filter blocks horizontal rays.

Polarization
A polarizing filter is etched with tiny parallel lines, allowing light waves traveling only at a certain angle to pass through. The lenses of the glasses have different filters, so only one set of images reaches each eye.

Lenses direct light to the left eye.

Lenses direct light to the right eye.

Lenticular
This glasses-free 3-D method uses a screen coated with tiny lenses called lenticules. These bend the light coming from the screen, directing images to one eye or the other to build a 3-D view.

More here

CAVE 3-D TV stereoscope **polarized 3-D glasses** stereopsis lenticular TV screen

Search the web for the nearest IMAX theater, where exciting 3-D films are shown on huge screens.

The 3-D Center of Art and Photography in Portland, OR, is the world's first art gallery and museum dedicated to 3-D images.

  NINTENDO 3DS FACT FILE

Introduced: February 2011

3-D screen: 3.5 in. (9 cm)

Size: 5.3 in. x 2.9 in. x 0.8 in. (13.4 cm x 7.3 cm x 2 cm)

Weight: 8 oz. (226 g)

Worldwide sales: 6.7 million (as of October 2011)

lenticular lens: a curved lens that allows each eye to see a different image of the same object at exactly the same time.

stereoscopic 3-D: a system that uses two images, one for each eye, to create a 3-D effect.

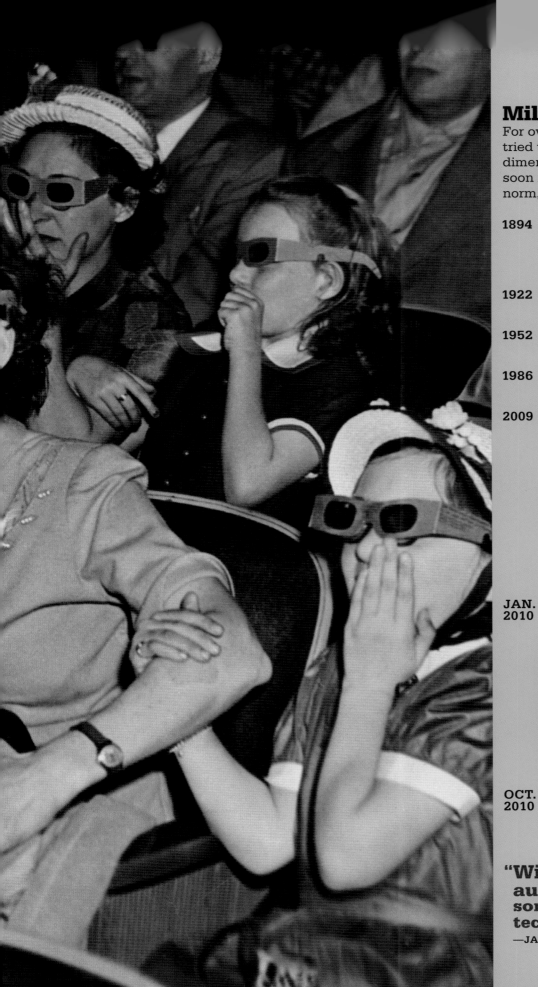

Milestones in 3-D

For over a century, inventors have tried to create realistic movies in three dimensions (3-D). Recent advances may soon make glasses-free 3-D viewing the norm, both at home and in theaters.

1894 ● British film pioneer William Friese-Greene patented a 3-D movie process, using a stereoscope (see page 50) to view two films shown side by side.

1922 ● *The Power of Love* was the first 3-D film shown to a paying audience.

1952 ● *Bwana Devil*, an adventure film, was the first 3-D movie in color.

1986 ● IMAX theaters showed the first 3-D documentaries on huge screens.

2009 ● A new kind of 3-D camera was used on the movie *Avatar* to give more depth to the 3-D scenes.

SCENE FROM *AVATAR* (2009)

JAN. 2010 ● Panasonic introduced the largest 3-D TV so far, with a screen measuring 152 inches (386 cm) diagonally.

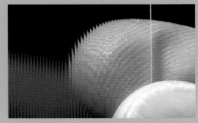

LENTICULAR SCREEN OF 3-D TV

OCT. 2010 ● Toshiba released the first glasses-free 3-D TV, which used a lenticular screen (see page 51).

"With 3-D projection . . . audiences will be seeing something that was never technically possible before!"
—JAMES CAMERON, DIRECTOR OF *AVATAR*

Sounds amazing

Sounds are waves of energy that travel away from the sound's source. From the 19th century onward, new technologies have provided different ways to capture and record sounds so that they can be stored and replayed later.

Gramophone
Invented in the 1890s, the gramophone replayed sounds held on flat discs. Called records, these discs stored analog sounds as tiny bumps and dips cut into a spiral groove on the disc.

Traveling sound
Sound waves travel as vibrations through a medium, such as air. Sounds vary in pitch (whether the tone is high or low) and in amplitude (the amount of energy the waves have). The greater the amplitude, the louder the sound will be when it reaches your ears.

HIGH-FREQUENCY WAVE

AMPLITUDE

TIME

LOW-FREQUENCY WAVE

Peak

Trough

Wavelength is the distance between troughs or peaks.

High or low?
Frequency is the number of waves per second. A greater frequency produces sound of a higher pitch.

MP3 files
The MP3 format is a way of storing digital sound files so that they take up less memory space. Software in a computer or MP3 player, such as an iPod, analyzes a track's sound waves and removes parts that are not needed.

AUDIO CD

Sound selection
Sounds that the human ear cannot hear are deleted by compression.

Storing more

Early gramophone records often had one track, or song, on each side of the disc. Here are the typical numbers of tracks on later storage formats.

14
Vinyl album *Long-playing (LP) records hold 52 minutes of sound.*

25
C90 cassette *A reel of magnetic tape inside stores 1.5 hours of audio.*

940% increase

2004   2009

Download

Digital downloads
The market for digital music downloads boomed between 2004 and 2009. Legal downloaded digital music sales worldwide in 2010 totaled more than $4.6 billion.

Loudness
The decibel scale is a measure of the intensity, or loudness, of a sound. A sound that is 10 decibels greater than another sound is 10 times louder. So a 20-decibel increase is 100 times louder (10 x 10), and a 30-decibel increase is 1,000 times louder (10 x 10 x 10).

Near and far
Here are some typical sounds and their ratings on the decibel scale when heard from nearby. Sounds lose energy and loudness the farther they have to travel.

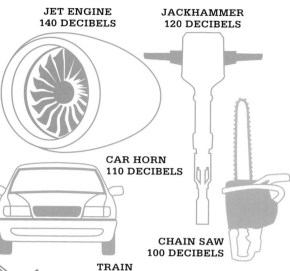

JET ENGINE
140 DECIBELS

JACKHAMMER
120 DECIBELS

CAR HORN
110 DECIBELS

CHAIN SAW
100 DECIBELS

TRAIN
80 DECIBELS

WHISPER
40 DECIBELS

WIND TURBINE
50 DECIBELS

HAIR DRYER
90 DECIBELS

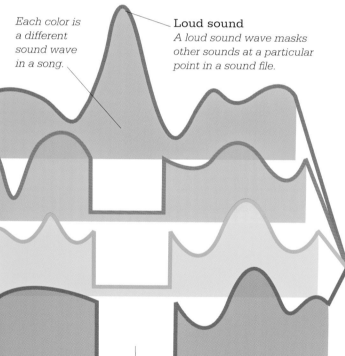

Each color is a different sound wave in a song.

Loud sound
A loud sound wave masks other sounds at a particular point in a sound file.

Space saver
Sounds masked by a loud sound are not included in the MP3 file.

How compression works
Compression removes very high- or low-pitched sounds beyond the range of human hearing, and also those masked, or covered, by louder sounds. The resulting MP3 file may be 90 percent smaller than the original.

MP3 PLAYER

iPod
Sounds are stored as digital data files in an iPod's memory. When replayed, a sound processor and digital-to-analog converter chips turn the digital data back into sound waves.

iPod

312 million iPods were sold by mid-2011

MENU

22

CD *One-sided compact discs hold up to 80 minutes of sound.*

1,000

DVD *A digital versatile disc can store up to 4.7 gigabytes of data.*

40,000

160GB MP3 player
This can play a new song every day for 109 years.

Electric guitar

In the 1930s, the invention of the electric guitar changed music forever. This new technology ushered in rock, indie, punk, metal, and many more new styles. Played unplugged, an electric guitar is quiet. Its vibrating strings need electrical amplification to really rock!

Strings
Each string is of a different thickness, so each produces different notes.

Pickup covers

Pickups
A pickup detects the vibrations of the strings (see opposite page). Below each string is a permanent magnet; the six magnets are wrapped in a coil of copper wire.

Pickguard
Usually made of plastic, this thin sheet protects the guitar's body from scratches.

Fender Stratocaster
Green Day lead guitarist Billie Joe Armstrong plays a Fender Stratocaster. First made in 1954, the "Strat" has been played by many great guitarists, including Jimi Hendrix and U2's The Edge.

Volume control
Turning this knob increases or decreases the volume.

VOLUME
8 9 10 1 2 3

TONE
8 9 10 1 2 3

TONE
1 2 3 4 5 6

Anatomy of a guitar
Like other electric guitars, the Fender Stratocaster has six strings made of metal wire. They are held taut between the bridge and the tuning pegs. The harder a string is struck, the more it vibrates—and the louder the sound it makes when plugged into an amplifier.

Metal bridge
The strings attach here, supported by six small grooves called saddles.

Strap hook
The guitar's shoulder strap attaches to this hook.

Jack socket
This is where you plug in the jack lead—the cable that connects the guitar to an amplifier.

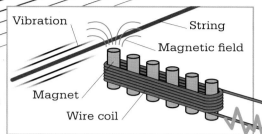

Vibration · String · Magnetic field · Magnet · Wire coil · Signal from pickup · Electrical signal

How pickups work

When a guitar string is played, its vibration disturbs the force field produced by the magnet beneath it. This causes an electric current to flow through the wire coil.

Signal from pickup

A signal in the form of a varying electric current is sent through the guitar's wiring to the jack socket.

Tuning pegs

These geared pegs can be turned to alter the strings' pitch.

Headstock

The wooden head holds the tuning pegs.

4,000 ft.

(1,220 m): the length of the copper wire in the coil of a typical guitar pickup

Fretboard

Pressing the fingers down here changes the length of each string, and its pitch.

Pickup selector

This switch determines which pickups are used. Each pickup gives a distinctive sound.

Tone controls

Turning up the knobs gives a "brighter" sound with more treble.

Wooden body

With a body made of wood such as alder, maple, or ash, an electric guitar typically weighs 6.5–11 pounds (3–5 kg).

Control cavity

Parts of the body are hollowed out to hold the wiring from the guitar's pickups and the controls to the jack socket.

Pump up the volume

The signal from an electric guitar needs to be boosted in power. An amplifier receives the signal, increases its strength, and sends it to a loudspeaker. The loudspeaker converts the signal back into sounds, which are louder than those originally made by the strings.

Strengthened signal from amplifier

SIGNAL FROM GUITAR

AMPLIFIER

Weak signal from guitar

Signal in

The electrical signal enters the metal coil.

Metal coil

The coil becomes an electromagnet, creating a changing magnetic field.

Loudspeaker

Sound waves travel out from the loudspeaker as vibrations in the air.

Cone

The moving coil causes the cone to vibrate, generating sound waves.

Movement

The permanent magnet and the electromagnet attract and repel each other, making the coil move.

Permanent magnet

Roller coasters [The rides

When you visit a theme park, you'll find the longest lines at the roller coasters. These rides are closed circuits of twisting, dipping tracks on which cars carrying thrill seekers whiz by at high speeds. Strap yourself in and check out this nerve-shredding selection of coasters.

Strata

Roller coasters with drops totaling over 400 feet (120 m) are called strata coasters. Only two have been built so far, the taller of which is Kingda Ka (below).

Name	Kingda Ka, Six Flags Great Adventure, US
Cool fact	Highest point is 456 ft. (139 m)
Introduced	2005

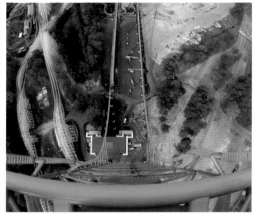

Launch

Powerful electric motors or hydraulic (pressurized-liquid) systems can launch riders to superfast speeds almost instantly. Dodonpa (left), in Japan, uses another launch method—compressed air—to send riders racing down its 3,901-foot (1,189 m) track.

Name	Dodonpa, Fuji-Q Highland, Japan
Cool fact	0–107 mph (0–172 kph) in 1.8 seconds
Introduced	2001

Hair-raising high-rise
Dodonpa's cars are propelled over a vertical part of the track that is as high as a 17-story building.

Dizzying drop
This picture shows the view from the "top hat" hill of Kingda Ka, featuring a fearsome drop longer than a football field.

Cable lift

Many rides, including El Toro (below), start with a slow rise to the highest part of the track, with the cars hauled up by winch or cable systems. Then they plummet down a steep slope, powered by gravity.

Name	El Toro, Six Flags Great Adventure, US
Cool fact	Wooden, with a 76-degree slope
Introduced	2006

Fastest

Formula Rossa, in Abu Dhabi's Ferrari World theme park, is the fastest roller coaster in the world. Riders wear protective glasses as their cars roar from 0 to 62 mph (0 to 100 kph) in just 2 seconds.

FORMULA ROSSA

150 mph (240 kph): the maximum speed Formula Rossa reaches along its 1.3-mile (2.1 km) course

Terrifying Toro
As the cars hurtle down the slope, they build up enough speed to carry them around the rest of the ride.

Flying

Suspended in horizontal positions like flying superheroes, riders on these coasters are flung around swooping turns and soaring lifts.

Name	Flying Coaster, Genting, Malaysia
Cool fact	Riders experience 3.6 times the force of gravity
Introduced	2004

Extreme force
On flying coasters, speeds are usually slower than 60 mph (96 kph), but thrills are high due to the unusual angle of the cars.

Inversion

On this type of ride, the passengers are suspended beneath the track on chairs or in pods. The chairs invert (flip upside down) on corkscrewing bends and turns, disorienting the riders. The UK's Nemesis (above) was the first inversion roller coaster in Europe.

Name	Nemesis, Alton Towers, UK
Cool fact	The ride includes 4 inversions
Introduced	1994

Midair inversion
Nemesis passengers are flipped over in midair during their thrilling 2,349-foot (716 m) ride, which also passes through an underground tunnel.

Theme-park thrills

Riders hurtle along at up to 62 miles per hour (100 kph) on the Tatsu roller coaster at Six Flags Magic Mountain in California. Designed and modeled with computers, cutting-edge rides use sudden acceleration and changes in angle to serve up serious thrills. Passengers are launched at high speed, looped upside down, and hurled around the track's corkscrewing twists.

Force, s
pow

* Do Jet Skis use jet engines?

* How does a space rocket overcome Earth's gravity?

* Which car smashed the sound barrier?

peed, &
wer

Engines and motors

Flick a switch, turn a key, or push a button, and machines burst into life. It's all thanks to engines and motors—devices that convert fuel or electrical energy into force and movement.

3,000 lb. (1,360 kg) of air is drawn into a GE90 jet engine every second

Internal combustion engine

Most cars are powered by internal combustion engines. A mixture of fuel and air is burned in the engine's cylinders, forcing pistons up and down. A crankshaft changes this motion into a turning movement that drives the car's wheels.

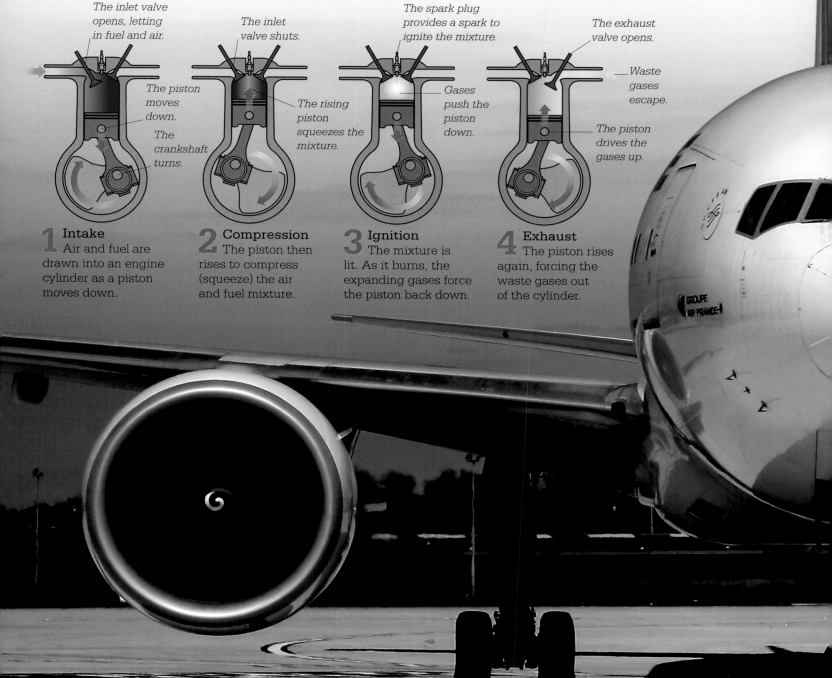

The inlet valve opens, letting in fuel and air.

The piston moves down.

The crankshaft turns.

The inlet valve shuts.

The rising piston squeezes the mixture.

The spark plug provides a spark to ignite the mixture.

Gases push the piston down.

The exhaust valve opens.

Waste gases escape.

The piston drives the gases up.

1 Intake
Air and fuel are drawn into an engine cylinder as a piston moves down.

2 Compression
The piston then rises to compress (squeeze) the air and fuel mixture.

3 Ignition
The mixture is lit. As it burns, the expanding gases force the piston back down.

4 Exhaust
The piston rises again, forcing the waste gases out of the cylinder.

[The power providers]

Electric motor

Inside a motor is a wire coil surrounded by the force field of a magnet. When electricity flows through the coil, the coil produces its own magnetic field. The two fields push and pull on each other, making the coil rotate. This motion is used to power machinery.

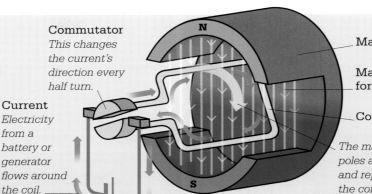

Commutator
This changes the current's direction every half turn.

Current
Electricity from a battery or generator flows around the coil.

Magnet

Magnetic force field

Coil

The magnet's poles attract and repel the coil.

How the coil turns
Magnetic attraction pulls the coil up on one side. When the commutator changes the direction of the current, the forces on the coil reverse. The coil is repelled, and pushed down on the other side.

Jet engine

The thrust (force) that pushes a jet aircraft forward is created by a stream of hot, high-speed, rapidly expanding gases that shoot from the rear of the engine.

Air intake
Cold air is drawn in at the front of the engine.

Combustion chamber
The air is mixed with fuel and ignited in the combustion chamber.

Parts of a jet engine
Fuel is burned in the combustion chamber. The compressor and turbine are linked by a shaft.

Rotating crankshaft

Compressor
A series of spinning fans compresses the air and forces it backward.

Turbine
Turned by expanding waste gases as they escape, this set of bladed wheels drives the compressor.

Exhaust nozzle
Waste gases zoom out of the nozzle much faster than air enters the engine.

World's biggest jet engine
Each mighty GE90-115B engine on this Boeing 777-300ER airliner is able to produce up to 127,900 lb. (58,000 kg) of thrust.

Supercar [Fast and furious]

The Bugatti Veyron is one of the world's most desirable supercars. These high-tech sports cars offer the ultimate in performance and style, but at a high price. The Veyron, which holds the road car records for speed and acceleration, can cost up to $2.4 million.

Veyron 16.4 specifications	
Made by	Bugatti, France
Introduced	2005
Engine 16 cylinders; 1,050 horsepower	
0–62 mph (0–100 kph)	2.5 seconds
0–124 mph (0–200 kph)	7.3 seconds
0–186 mph (0–300 kph)	16.7 seconds
Top speed	267 mph (431 kph)
Braking: 248–0 mph (400–0 kph)	Less than 10 seconds

Streamlined car
The curved shape lets air pass smoothly over the car.

Car body
The strong yet lightweight carbon-fiber body is about 14.5 ft. (4.5 m) long and 4 ft. (1.2 m) high.

Seats
The leather-covered seats contain heaters to warm them up on cold days.

BUGATTI BRESCIA, 1925

Racing heritage
Founded in 1909 in France, Bugatti has a long history of making ultrafast cars with powerful engines. In the 1920s and 1930s, Bugatti cars won more than 2,000 races.

Powerful performer

The Veyron is built by hand in Alsace, France. Its engine produces up to eight times the power of a typical sedan car's. The suspension, engine, and other systems (including the air pressure in each tire) are computer controlled, ensuring that the car always gives peak performance.

Tires
Special "run-flat" tires can be driven on even if punctured.

Wheels
The 20-in. (50 cm) wheels are made of a metal mixture called an alloy.

Gearshift
The driver changes gears using small paddlelike switches on the steering wheel.

Turbochargers
Four turbochargers boost the engine's power.

Driveshaft
This transfers power from the engine to all four wheels.

Gearbox
This contains seven gears, each of which changes the speed of the driveshaft and the amount of force it turns with.

Spoiler
The spoiler acts as a brake at high speeds, and it also produces a downward force to help keep the car on the road.

Air ducts
Openings in the roof let air flow into the rear of the car to help cool the brakes and the engine.

Crash protection
Some Veyrons have side-impact bars in the doors to protect the driver and passengers in a broadside collision.

Fuel tank
Made of 250 parts, the tank holds about 26 gal. (100 L) of fuel.

Engine pistons
The 16 pistons are arranged in 4 angled rows. Each moves up and down inside its own cylinder.

Speed on the road
The sleek lines of a Bugatti Veyron help it travel at top speed. Above 137 mph (200 kph), the body automatically lowers over the wheels to help grip the road.

2.3 seconds: how long it takes for a Veyron to brake from 62 mph (100 kph) to a complete standstill

Compact engine
The Veyron's compact but powerful internal combustion engine (see page 64) burns fuel in 16 cylinders.

Heat-resistant brakes
The brake discs must withstand the extreme heat produced by friction when braking at high speed.

Power booster
A turbocharger squashes the air entering an engine so that more is forced into the cylinders. This enables extra fuel to be burned, increasing the power output.

Compressor

Linking shaft

Turbine

Air is drawn into the turbocharger.

Exhaust gases from burning fuel in the cylinder are released.

Compressed air

Piston

Engine cylinder

A cooler ensures that the air is at the right temperature.

How it works
The engine's exhaust gases turn a set of blades called a turbine. The rotating turbine spins a wheel called a compressor. This draws in air and compresses (squashes) it before the air enters the cylinders.

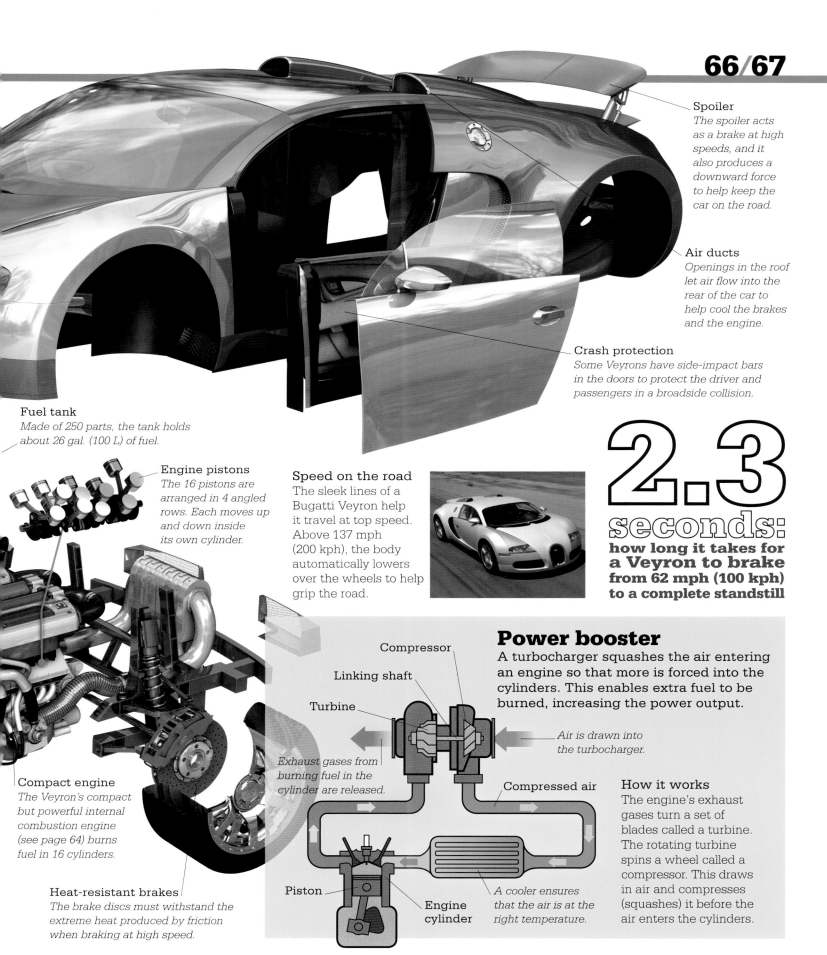

Cars [Technology in motion]

Developed in the late 19th century, the earliest automobiles were slow, unreliable, and difficult to control, but they started the transport revolution. Today, over 500 million motor vehicles carry people and goods in every country around the globe.

1885
Gasoline-powered car
German engineer Karl Benz's Motorwagen was the first car with an internal combustion engine (see page 64). The engine burned gasoline and air to generate power.

BENZ MOTORWAGEN

1938
The "people's car"
In Germany, work began on the Volkswagen ("people's car"). Nicknamed the Beetle, this simple, affordable car was made in huge numbers—over 21 million were built between 1938 and 2003.

VOLKSWAGEN BEETLE

1769
In France, Nicolas-Joseph Cugnot built a three-wheeled, steam-powered wagon that moved at walking speed.

1912
US policeman Lester Wire invented the first electric traffic lights, with red for stop and green for go.

1934
In the UK, "cat's eye" road studs were patented. Cat's eyes reflect headlights to show drivers the way ahead on dark roads.

•1770 — •1900 — •1920 — •1950

Dots represent 10-year increases.

1891
France's Michelin brothers patented a pneumatic (air-filled) tire that, when punctured, could be taken off the wheel and repaired.

1912
The electric ignition was developed in the US by Charles Kettering, enabling cars to be started without turning a crank.

1963
Swedish manufacturer Volvo became the first to equip its cars with seat belts.

1908
Ford Model T
Henry Ford's Model T was the first car to be mass-produced on a moving assembly line in a factory. The cheap, reliable Model T led to a boom in car ownership.

FORD MODEL T ASSEMBLY LINE, HIGHLAND PARK, MICHIGAN, 1913

1949
Sierra Sam
Sam was the first crash-test dummy—a life-size doll with sensors to test how accidents impact the body. These tests can make vehicles safer.

CRASH-TEST DUMMIES

20 mph (32 kph): the maximum speed limit imposed in the UK by the 1903 Motor Car Act

1987
Ferrari F40
The F40 was the first road car to reach 200 miles per hour (322 kph). It was created to commemorate the 40th anniversary of the founding of the Ferrari car company by Enzo Ferrari, a former racing driver.

ENZO FERRARI

Italian manufacturer

Founded:	Ferrari S.p.A.
Developed:	Fast, stylish cars

1979
First monster truck
The monster truck Bigfoot was introduced in the United States. Monster trucks, such as Samson (above), have giant wheels and powerful suspensions. They can climb over large obstacles like old cars in races and shows.

1981
Mercedes-Benz S-Class cars were fitted with an air bag that inflated to protect the driver in a crash.

2005
The Bugatti Veyron, the world's fastest sports car, was launched. Top speed: 253 mph (407 kph).

Dots represent 5-year increases.

·1975 ·1990 ·2000

1972
The antilock braking system (ABS) was invented by Bosch in Germany. It keeps brakes from locking and causing skidding.

1974
Catalytic converters were introduced in the US. A "cat" removes some of the toxins from exhaust gases.

1997
The Toyota Prius—a "hybrid" car that has both a gasoline engine and an electric motor—made its debut.

1998
The Smart Car was first sold in Europe. With a small engine and only two seats, it is designed for short trips in towns and cities.

1988
Head-up display
The Oldsmobile Cutlass Supreme was the first car with a head-up display (HUD). HUDs beam an image of the dash instruments onto the windshield, so the driver doesn't have to look down.

HEAD-UP DISPLAY ON A SPORTS CAR

48:
the number of lithium-ion batteries **that power the Nissan LEAF to its top speed of 90 mph (145 kph)**

2010
Electric family car
The Nissan LEAF electric car went on sale in Japan and the United States. It can travel over 60 miles (100 km) on one charge, and it emits no waste gas.

NISSAN LEAF

Extreme speed [Smashing

Meet the vehicles for which extreme speed is routine. The fastest vehicles in their class, these are the results of many years of development and testing. Constant improvements to their power and aerodynamics have turned them into machines that can slice through the air at maximum velocity.

Sikorsky X2

Hovering is easy for helicopters, but few fly faster than 200 mph (322 kph). In 2010, aided by an extra push from its rear propeller, the Sikorsky X2 set a new record of 299 mph (481 kph).

What it is	Fastest helicopter
Built by	Sikorsky, United States
Introduced	2008

SR-71 Blackbird

Designed to fly high and fast to spy on enemies below, the SR-71 is the fastest jet aircraft ever made. In 1976, one zoomed to a top speed of 2,193 mph (3,530 kph). It was retired from service in 1998.

What it is	Fastest jet aircraft
Built by	Lockheed, United States
Introduced	1966

High-flying Blackbird
An SR-71 soars high over the Sierra Nevada mountains, California. The jet could climb to 80,258 ft. (24,390 m).

Twinset
The X2 research helicopter has two sets of rotors, one above the other.

Suzuki Hayabusa

The Hayabusa's engine is as big as a hatchback car's, but it is engineered to produce much more power. This superbike has reached speeds of up to 194 mph (312 kph).

What it is	Fastest road motorcycle
Built by	Suzuki, Japan
Introduced	1999

Awesome acceleration
The Hayabusa can go from 0 to 60 mph (0 to 96 kph) in less than 3 seconds.

Rocket sled

In 1954, John Stapp of the US Air Force became the fastest man on Earth. The rocket sled he was strapped to propelled him along at 632 mph (1,017 kph). That's faster than a bullet shot from a revolver!

Sonic Wind No. 1
Stapp's sled, called Sonic Wind No. 1, traveled along rails. The sled was used to research human safety at high speeds.

CRH380A

Racing along specially built tracks at 221 mph (355 kph), China's CRH380A electric trains link the cities of Shanghai, Nanjing, and Hangzhou. On a test run in 2010, a CRH380A went 302 mph (486 kph)—a record for a wheeled rail vehicle. (John Stapp's rocket sled went faster—see above.)

What it is	Fastest wheeled rail vehicle
Built by	CSR, China
Introduced	2010

Long haul
China's CRH380A locomotive pulls eight passenger cars, each with up to 85 riders.

Big burners
Mounted on either side of the driver's cockpit, ThrustSSC's immense jet engines burned around 4.8 gallons (18 L) of fuel every second!

771 mph
(1,241 kph):
the top speed achieved by ThrustSSC in 1997, in the Black Rock Desert, Nevada

ThrustSSC
Powered by two jet engines (see page 65) normally used in Phantom military planes, ThrustSSC set a new world land speed record in 1997. Over two runs, it averaged 763 mph (1,229 kph).

What it is	Fastest land vehicle
Built by	ThrustSSC Project, United Kingdom
Introduced	1996

Breaking the sound barrier
ThrustSSC was the first "car" to go faster than sound. Here, it creates a shock wave as it breaks the sound barrier in the Nevada desert.

Racing powerboat

A Formula 1 powerboat momentarily takes to the air off the coast of Kiev, Ukraine. A 425-horsepower engine thrusts the boat's lightweight carbon-fiber hull over the water's surface with great force. Powerboats are phenomenally fast. They can accelerate from a standstill to 100 mph (160 kph) in 4 seconds and can reach a top speed of just over 130 mph (225 kph).

Takeoff [Getting airborne]

Planes and helicopters are heavy. The heaviest of all, the Antonov An-225 cargo plane, has a maximum takeoff weight of 640 tons. So how do aircraft get off the ground and into the air? The answer is a force called lift.

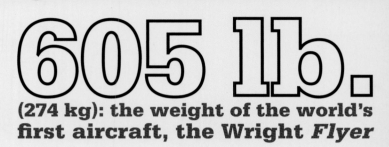

605 lb.
(274 kg): the weight of the world's first aircraft, the Wright *Flyer*

Airplanes

To start an airplane down the runway, its engine must produce enough thrust to overcome a force called drag, which resists forward movement. As the plane increases in speed, the flow of air around its wings generates an upward force called lift. When lift exceeds the weight of the plane, the aircraft rises into the air.

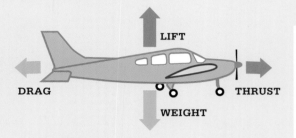

LIFT

DRAG   THRUST

WEIGHT

Forces on an aircraft
To take off, thrust must be greater than drag, and lift must exceed weight. Once airborne, the aircraft flies level if the forces remain equal.

Airbus A380
This 853-seat airliner, the world's largest plane, has four jet engines. Its 260-foot (80 m) wingspan gives a huge amount of lift.

Airfoils

Wings are airfoils—structures that are curved on top but flatter underneath. An airfoil is angled so that it pushes air downward, and its shape creates an area of higher pressure below the wing. These two actions create lift.

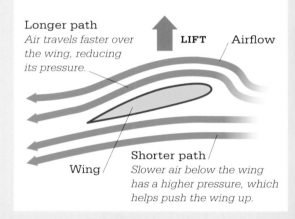

Longer path
Air travels faster over the wing, reducing its pressure.

LIFT — Airflow

Wing

Shorter path
Slower air below the wing has a higher pressure, which helps push the wing up.

Helicopters

The main blades of a helicopter are long airfoils. Driven by the engine, they spin fast, often at a rate of 300 turns per minute. The speed of the blades and their angle can be altered by the pilot to create more or less lift.

Landing area
Helicopters need only a small space to land, such as on the landing pad of this oil rig.

Rotor blades
The main blades are attached to a rotor head. They produce lift as they spin, so the helicopter rises vertically.

Tail rotor
The rear rotors balance the turning forces created by the main blades.

Moving forward
The rotor head tilts so that the blades drive air backward as well as down.

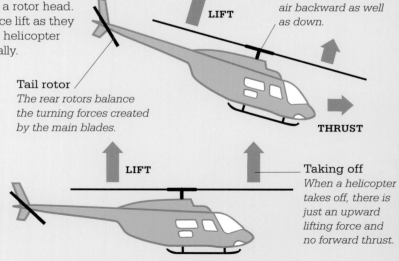

LIFT

THRUST

LIFT   LIFT

Taking off
When a helicopter takes off, there is just an upward lifting force and no forward thrust.

Vertical takeoff
The Sea Harrier is designed to fly from aircraft carriers. It is a VTOL plane, capable of vertical takeoff and landing. Taking off vertically uses a lot of fuel, so the Harrier often takes off conventionally. It speeds along the carrier's flight deck and makes use of a ramp at the end.

Directing thrust
This computer simulation shows how the Harrier's rotating jet-engine nozzles direct their thrust downward for a vertical takeoff. Once airborne, the nozzles swivel to point behind, pushing the aircraft forward.

Surface skimmers [Riding

Any boat moving through water is slowed down by a resisting force called drag. Craft that move over the top of the water keep drag to a minimum, so they can travel faster or carry greater loads.

63.5 mph
(102 kph): the top speed of the Yamaha WaveRunner FX Cruiser

Jet Skis

Jet Skis are the motorcycles of the water—fast and exciting as they skim the waves. Steered with handlebars, they are pushed along by powerful jets of water. Riders can also lean into turns, just like motorcyclists can.

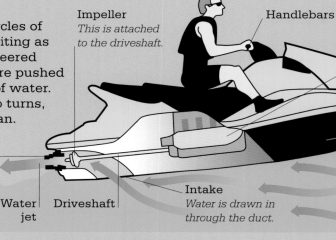

Impeller
This is attached to the driveshaft.

Handlebars

Engine
A gas engine rapidly spins the driveshaft.

Steering nozzle
The nozzle, turned by the handlebars, alters the direction of thrust.

Water jet

Driveshaft

Intake
Water is drawn in through the duct.

Propeller
A boat's curved, spinning propeller blades force water backward, which pushes the boat forward through the water. Airplane propellers work in the same way in air.

Impeller power
The impeller—a propeller enclosed in a tube called a duct—spins fast to draw in water from under the Jet Ski. The water is then forced out from the nozzle at the rear as a high-pressure jet.

Mighty machine
The powerful Yamaha WaveRunner FX Cruiser is made of ultra-lightweight but high-strength material. This improves its acceleration and makes it easier to handle. It can carry the driver and two passengers.

Hovercraft

These craft are amphibious—able to travel over both water and land. They have fans to generate lift (see page 74) and propellers for thrust. Fins called rudders, positioned in the flow of air behind the propellers, steer the craft.

Cushion of air
The rubber skirt around the base of the hovercraft holds in much of the air pushed underneath by the fans. This lifts the craft off the surface of the water.

Propeller
Pusher propellers at the rear drive the craft forward.

Lift fan
Large fans driven by the engine push air down with great force.

Flexible rubber skirt

Base of hovercraft

Escaping air
A little bit of air escapes, minimizing friction with the water or ground.

Air cushion
An area of high-pressure air forms under the hovercraft.

Car ferry
In service on the English Channel from 1968 to 2000, the SR.N4 was the biggest-ever commercial hovercraft. It carried up to 416 people and 60 cars.

Hydrofoils

At slow speeds, a hydrofoil travels like a regular boat, with its hull in the water. At high speeds, the hull rises above the surface, supported by winglike foils. A propeller or an impeller (see opposite page) drives the boat along.

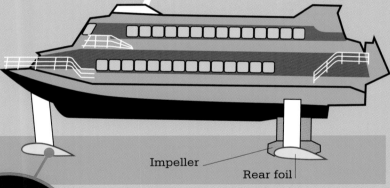

Impeller

Rear foil

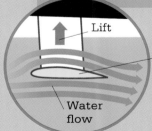

Lift

Front foil

Water flow

Underwater wings
Like airplane wings, the foils under the hull are airfoils (see page 74). At high speeds, the more rapid flow of water over the curved tops of the foils produces lift, raising the boat's hull out of the water.

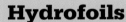

Jet-powered hydrofoil
Capable of reaching 52 mph (84 kph), the Boeing 929 Jetfoil is powered not by a propeller but by a water jet, somewhat like a Jet Ski is.

Escaping Earth [Blasting off]

Enormous power is needed to break free of Earth's gravity and head out into space. Rocket launch vehicles use rocket engines that carry their own fuel and oxidizer (source of oxygen). The fuel and oxygen are mixed together and burned to create vast amounts of thrust. The vehicle lifts off when the thrust is greater than the force of gravity pulling down on it.

Space shuttle liftoff
NASA's *Endeavour* space shuttle blasts off on its way to the International Space Station in 2009. The 528,000 gal. (2 million L) of fuel in the large orange fuel tank were used up during liftoff, so the tank was jettisoned (cast off) just nine minutes after launch.

All shapes and sizes

The first-ever liquid-fueled rocket was just 11.2 ft. (3.4 m) tall and weighed 6 lb. (2.7 kg). Modern rockets have to be large enough to carry heavy payloads (cargo such as satellites) and need huge quantities of fuel and oxidizer.

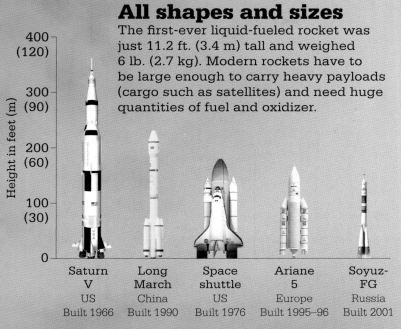

Height in feet (m)

400 (120)
300 (90)
200 (60)
100 (30)
0

Saturn V — US — Built 1966
Long March — China — Built 1990
Space shuttle — US — Built 1976
Ariane 5 — Europe — Built 1995–96
Soyuz-FG — Russia — Built 2001

Biggest-ever launch vehicles
Saturn V rockets launched all the Apollo missions to the Moon between 1968 and 1972. The rockets stood 363 ft. (110 m) tall—60 ft. (18 m) taller than the Statue of Liberty.

Liquid-fueled rocket

Many rocket engines use a liquid fuel such as hydrogen, gasoline, or kerosene. A Saturn V F-1 engine uses 1,733 lb. (788 kg) of liquid hydrogen every second.

Intense heat
The rocket engine has to withstand temperatures of up to 5,800°F (3,227°C).

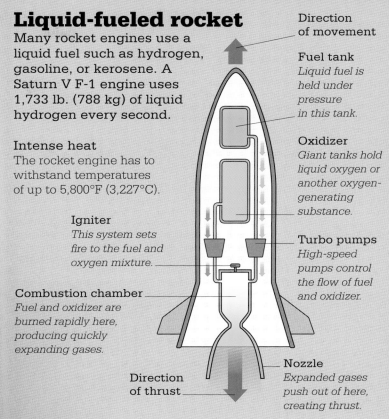

Direction of movement

Fuel tank
Liquid fuel is held under pressure in this tank.

Oxidizer
Giant tanks hold liquid oxygen or another oxygen-generating substance.

Igniter
This system sets fire to the fuel and oxygen mixture.

Turbo pumps
High-speed pumps control the flow of fuel and oxidizer.

Combustion chamber
Fuel and oxidizer are burned rapidly here, producing quickly expanding gases.

Direction of thrust

Nozzle
Expanded gases push out of here, creating thrust.

Rocket launch

The heavier the launch vehicle, the more fuel has to be burned to create the thrust needed. One solution is a multistage rocket—each stage (tank) is jettisoned, falling away once its fuel is used up.

Ariane 5
This is a typical launch pattern for the European Space Agency's Ariane 5 rocket.

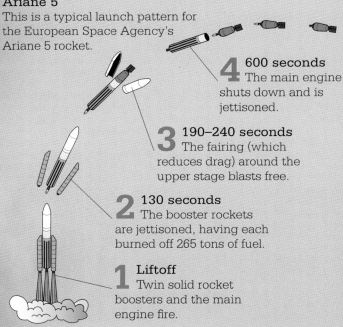

4 **600 seconds** The main engine shuts down and is jettisoned.

3 **190–240 seconds** The fairing (which reduces drag) around the upper stage blasts free.

2 **130 seconds** The booster rockets are jettisoned, having each burned off 265 tons of fuel.

1 **Liftoff** Twin solid rocket boosters and the main engine fire.

Launching astronauts in rockets is only one way to explore space. Much of what we know about the Universe comes from telescopes and from robotic space probes that can endure conditions too hostile for humans.

Looking into space

Optical telescopes capture light. Other telescopes gather different forms of energy given off by objects in space, including X-rays and radio waves. Below are some examples of what can be seen from Earth and from telescopes in space. One light-year (ly) is about 6 trillion miles (9.6 trillion km).

2.5 million light-years

Naked eye
The Andromeda galaxy, 2.5 million ly away, is visible by eye on a cloudless night.

54 million light-years

Home telescope
Telescopes reveal more, including M87, a giant galaxy 54 million ly away containing a trillion stars.

600 million light-years

Parkes (radio)
Australia's Parkes telescope has detected radio waves from Cygnus A, a galaxy 600 million ly away.

10.2 billion light-years

Chandra (X-ray)
This orbiting observatory has identified a group of galaxies, JKCS041, around 10.2 billion ly from Earth.

13.2 billion light-years

Hubble (optical)
From its position high above Earth, Hubble has observed the farthest known stars, over 13.2 billion ly away.

Space probes

These unpiloted craft explore the solar system, sending data back to Earth by radio signal. Some fly by their target, measuring it as they go. Others go into orbit around a moon or planet, or even land on it.

MESSENGER
Target: Mercury (launched 2004)
Distance from Earth: 96 million miles
(155 million km) in 2011

Long-distance
Over time, some probes travel vast distances through space.

SUN   MERCURY   VENUS   EARTH   MARS

SMART-1
Target: the Moon (launched 2003)
Distance from Earth: 230,600 miles
(380,000 km)

Last men on the Moon
Using their lunar rover, Eugene Cernan and Harrison Schmitt of Apollo 17 collected 245 lb. (111 kg) of Moon rock. They were the last of 12 astronauts who walked on the Moon between 1969 and 1972.

Space junk

Orbiting Earth at an average speed of 17,400 mph (28,000 kph) are millions of bits of debris from space missions. They range from flecks of paint to rocket parts.

Astro-trash
The many items of space junk include a lost camera, glove, and tool kit, as well as garbage bags.

19,000
pieces of space junk are larger than 4 in. (10 cm)

Space suits

In Earth orbit, spacewalking astronauts face temperatures ranging from −250°F (−157°C) to over 275°F (135°C). They need tough protective suits with built-in life-support systems—and room to grow!

life-support system
The pack includes oxygen tanks, cooling equipment, a radio, and a battery for electrical power.

plastic visor
The visor has a thin gold coating to block the Sun's harmful ultraviolet rays.

Suited and booted
All the suit's parts interlock so that no skin is exposed. The suit weighs about 280 lb. (127 kg) on Earth, but in space it is weightless.

2 in

1 in

Growing taller
Without gravity pulling the spine down, the body gets about 2 in. (5 cm) taller.

gloves
Heated fingertips keep fingers from going numb while working in space.

layers
The suit has 14 layers. Some keep the body at the right temperature. Others protect against tiny space rocks called micrometeoroids.

New Horizons
*Target: Pluto (launched 2006)
Distance from Earth: 3 billion miles (4.8 billion km) in 2015*

Asteroid belt

JUPITER   SATURN   URANUS   NEPTUNE   PLUTO

Rosetta
*Target: Comet 67P (launched 2004)
Distance from Earth: 406 million miles (654 million km) in 2014*

Pioneer 10
*Target: Jupiter (launched 1972)
Distance from Earth: 7.5 billion miles (12 billion km)*

Voyager 1
*Target: deep space (launched 1977)
Distance from Earth: 10.8 billion miles (17.4 billion km)*

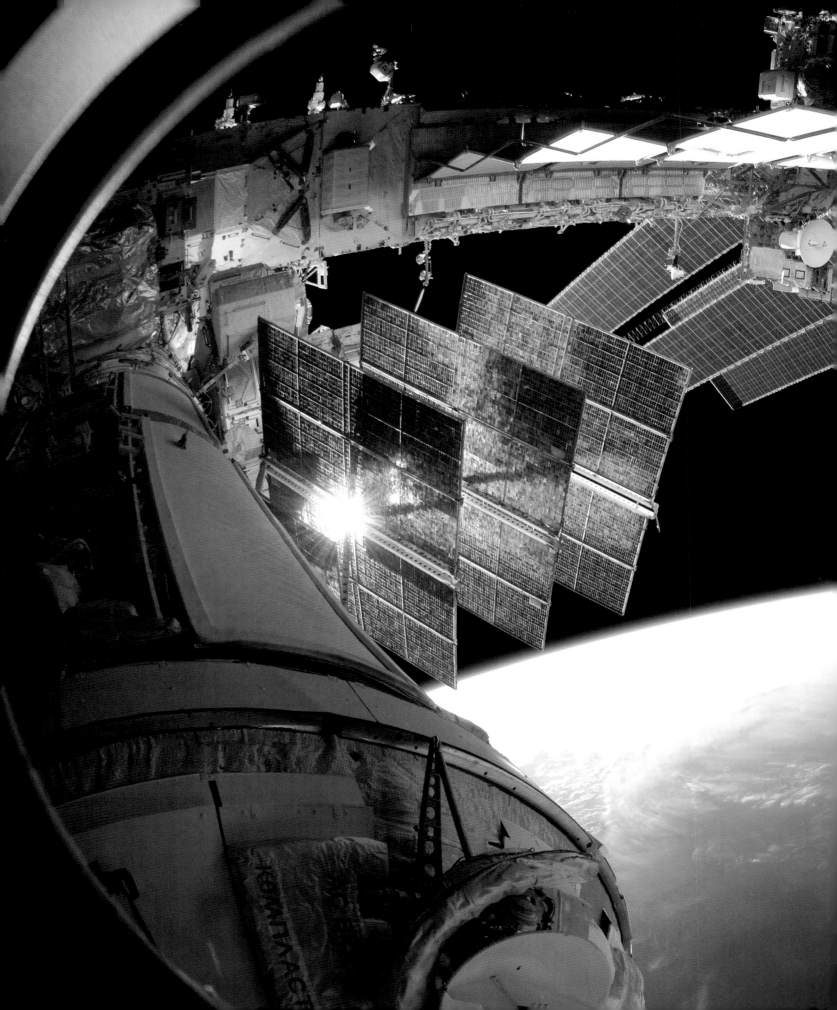

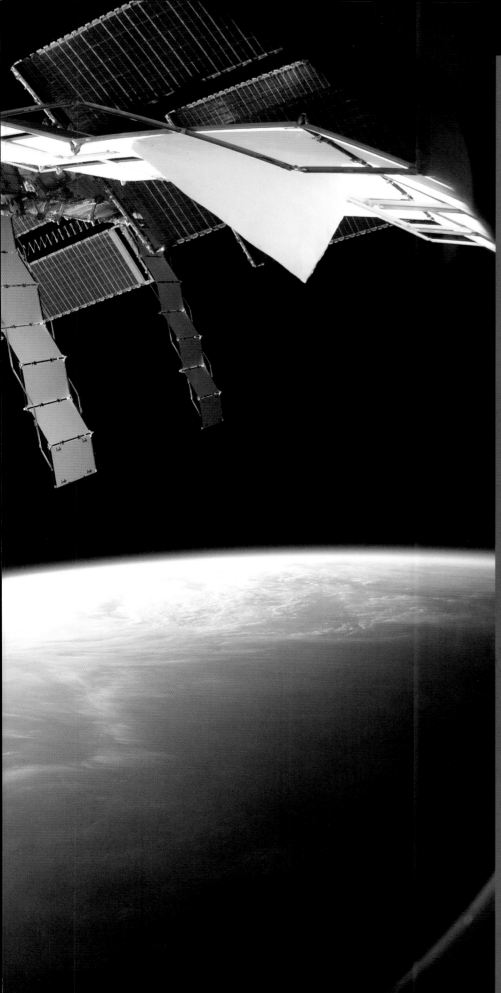

Construction in space

The International Space Station (ISS) is an orbiting base for scientific research. It circles Earth more than 15 times each day, at an average altitude of 220 miles (354 km) above the planet's surface.

1998 The first module, Russia's Zarya—used for communications, power, and storage—was launched.

2000 With living quarters and a control center ready, the ISS received its first full-time crew of three astronauts.

2001 The Destiny science lab was added.

2002 The P1 and S1 parts of the ISS's truss—its giant spine—were fitted.

INSIDE KIBO LABORATORY

2008 The ISS gained a Japanese laboratory, Kibo; a European science module called Columbus; and Dextre, a giant, twin-armed Canadian robot.

2011 *Atlantis* made the 115th and final space shuttle visit to the ISS.

VIEW OF THE ISS IN 2011

2012 The ISS is scheduled to be complete and capable of running until 2020.

"This space station is the **pinnacle of human achievement and** international cooperation."
—GREG CHAMITOFF, ISS ASTRONAUT

Techn

for

* What is a solar furnace?

* When were the first color TV broadcasts?

* How do sneakers put an extra spring in your step?

ology
life

Mountain bike [Pedal power!]

Some bicycles are designed for cruising smooth city streets or riding along country lanes. But others, like this rugged mountain bike, give you the freedom to go off-road and tackle almost any terrain. Mountain bikes are built with specially designed materials that can withstand the jolts of a ride over rough ground.

"Penny-farthing" bicycles
Early bikes had no chain or gears, and the pedals were connected to the front wheel. The large wheel (the "penny") gave a smooth ride on uneven roads, steadied by the smaller "farthing."

On your bike
This lightweight mountain bike has full suspension, meaning that both the front and back wheels have suspension systems. It is designed to be ridden on bumpy trails or raced on off-road courses featuring hills, dips, rocks, and other obstacles.

Rear suspension
The air chamber acts like a spring, absorbing the force of hitting a bump. The oil and nitrogen chambers dampen the piston's movement as it returns to normal.

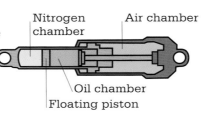

Nitrogen chamber

Air chamber

Oil chamber

Floating piston

Rubber tread
The chunky tread is designed to grip rough ground.

Beads
Metal rings called beads help to give the tire its shape.

Subtread
This tough inner layer protects the tire against punctures.

Disc brakes
When activated, pads press hard against a disc on the wheel. This creates friction, which slows down the wheel.

Rear fork

Downhill racing
On steep slopes, mountain bikes can reach over 50 mph (80 kph).

Gear derailleur
This mechanism directs the chain over the cog selected when the rider operates the gearshift.

Saddle
The seat is cushioned with gel pads to make the ride as comfortable as possible.

Lightweight frame
With carbon-fiber or aluminum-alloy frames, some mountain bikes weigh less than 24 lb. (10.9 kg).

Aluminum wheel and spokes

Gearshift

Rear suspension

Handlebars

Brake lever
This lever operates the hydraulic (pressurized-liquid) braking system.

Front suspension

Front suspension
Supported by springs, these tubes move up and down to cushion the rider over rough ground.

Air valve

Air chamber

Air piston

Spring

Lubrication oil

Lights
These lights contain several small but very bright light-emitting diode (LED) lamps to make a cyclist visible at night.

1.5 billion: the estimated number of bicycles on the world's roads in 2011

Gear cogs
The gear cassette on the rear wheel of this bike has ten different gear cogs, known as sprockets.

Bearings
These reduce friction.

Chainwheel

Crank

Chain and chainwheel
The chain connects the chainwheel to the cogs and transmits power from the pedals to the wheel.

MTB pedals
Mountain bike (MTB) shoes can be clipped into the pedals, allowing riders to generate power throughout the entire pedaling motion.

Head protection
A helmet reduces the chances of injuring your head if you crash. Most helmets consist of a hard plastic outer shell with a layer of thick expanded polystyrene foam inside.

Cool air in

Hard shell

Warm air out

The chin strap keeps the helmet in place.

Air vents
Holes channel air around a cyclist's head to keep it cool.

Structure
The crushable foam layer under the outer shell cushions the head. It absorbs much of the force of an impact.

Foam layer

Plastic outer shell

Radio-controlled racers

As model cars rev their electric motors (see page 65) before a race, each owner stands nearby, holding a radio-control transmitter. This device sends out radio-wave signals to the corresponding car's antenna. Electric circuits in the car convert the signals into commands and tell the motor to speed up, slow down, or reverse. Another motor, called a servo, steers the car by rotating precise amounts to turn it left or right.

Much of the energy that heats and lights our homes and powers our gadgets comes from burning fossil fuels (coal, oil, and gas). This creates pollution and releases carbon dioxide gas (CO_2), which is a cause of climate change. Saving energy reduces pollution, CO_2 in the air, and energy bills.

New gadgets

Many domestic electrical devices, such as PCs and game consoles, did not exist 30 years ago. Today, the amount of electricity that game consoles use in the US could power the city of San Diego, California.

Rapid change

In 1978, many US homes had washing machines, but big flat-screen TVs and DVD players had not yet been invented.

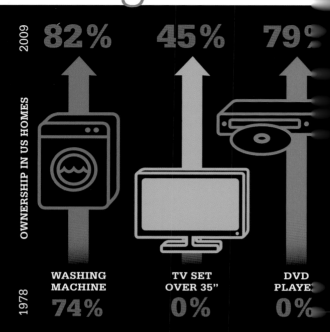

OWNERSHIP IN US HOMES

	WASHING MACHINE	TV SET OVER 35"	DVD PLAYER
2009	82%	45%	79%
1978	74%	0%	0%

World energy use

From 1900 to 2000, with the introduction of lots of new technology, the world's energy use increased by more than 10 times. However, the amount of energy used by people in different countries varies greatly.

Country		Annual energy use per person (lb)
India		1,199
China		3,516
United Kingdom		7,033
Germany		8,565
France		8,624
Australia		13,145
United States		15,565

ANNUAL ENERGY USE PER PERSON, IN POUNDS

Annual energy use

On average, each US citizen consumes nearly 13 times more energy than someone living in India.

KEY

= 1 BARREL, OR 770 LB. (350 KG), OF OIL, OR EQUIVALENT

Nuclear power 11.3%

Hydroelectricity 2.1%

Combustible renewables and waste 4.4%

Other: wind, solar, and geothermal power 1.1%

GAS 24.2%

OIL 37.2%

COAL 19.7%

Energy sources

Over 80 percent of the world's energy comes from the fossil fuels coal, oil, and natural gas, but they won't last forever.

Running out

The world is gradually using up its known reserves of coal, oil, and gas. Below are possible cutoff dates, if consumption does not lessen and no new reserves are found.

2055	2072	2128
OIL	NATURAL GAS	COAL

An average house in the US uses

30.16 kWh

of electricity each day

Helping the planet

We can reduce consumption of fossil fuels by using more energy-efficient devices, unplugging unused appliances, and installing technology that harnesses alternative energy sources, such as sunlight and wind (see pages 100–103).

Device	Photovoltaic panel
What it does	Sunlight makes electricity flow in the panel

Device	Wind turbine
What it does	Wind spins the blades, generating current

Device	Solar heating tube
What it does	Sunlight heats water in the tube

Alternative energy technology

Photovoltaic panels and wind turbines supply electricity for use in the home, while solar heating tubes provide hot water. All three devices are usually attached to roofs.

ELECTRIC KETTLE
2,000 W

Power ratings

The higher a device's power rating in watts (W) is, the more electricity it uses. Some devices use electricity even when they are in standby mode.

HAIR DRYER
1,000 W

25" COLOR TV
150 W

VIDEO GAME CONSOLE
80–90 W

60 W
TRADITIONAL INCANDESCENT BULB

13–15 W
COMPACT FLUORESCENT LAMP (CFL)

6–8 W
LIGHT-EMITTING DIODE (LED) BULB

Comparing lightbulb efficiency

Different bulbs of the same brightness have different power ratings (see right). LED bulbs use up to 10 times less electricity than incandescent ones.

Wattages
Domestic appliances have a wide range of power ratings. Those that heat water or air tend to use more electricity.

TABLE FAN
25 W

ELECTRIC SHAVER
15 W

If every US home replaced one incandescent bulb with a CFL, the energy saved could light
3 million houses

WASHING MACHINE
500 W

Domestic tech [A helping

Technology has transformed domestic life, bringing heat, light, new methods of preserving and preparing food, and entertainment to our homes. It has also given us labor-saving devices, such as dishwashers and vacuum cleaners, that help make daily tasks less of a chore.

1876
Telephone
In Boston, Alexander Graham Bell, a Scottish-born inventor, made the first telephone voice call. Later the same year, he made the first two-way long-distance phone call.

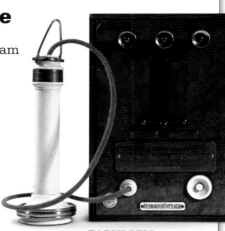

EARLY BELL TELEPHONE, 1877

ca. 100 BCE
Central heating
The ancient Romans invented an under-floor central heating system called a hypocaust. Hot air from a furnace warmed rooms as it passed through gaps in the walls and spaces below the raised floors.

UNDER-FLOOR HEATING AT A ROMAN VILLA

1902
In the US, Willis Haviland Carrier built the first electric air-conditioning system. It was installed in a printing factory.

1909
Frank Shailor patented the first commercially successful electric toaster in the US.

Dots represent 10-year increases.

100 BCE   **1500**   **1870**

Dots represent 100-year increases.

ca. 3000–2700 BCE
Plumbing pipes to carry water to and from houses were developed by the Indus Valley civilization (in modern-day Pakistan).

ca. 710 BCE
The oldest known lock and key were installed at the palace of Sargon II, ruler of Assyria (now part of Iraq).

1886
Josephine Cochrane of Ohio designed a mechanical dishwasher to keep her servants from breaking dishes while washing them.

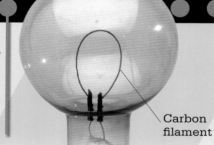

Carbon filament

1596
Flushing toilet
Sir John Harrington, the godson of England's Queen Elizabeth I, designed and installed a flushing mechanical "water closet," or toilet, in his manor house.

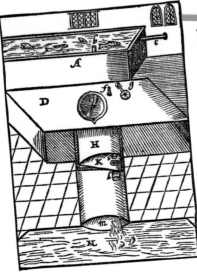

DIAGRAM OF HARRINGTON'S TOILET

1878–79
Electric lightbulb
American inventor Thomas Edison developed the first commercially successful lightbulb. A filament (thin strand) of carbon glowed with light when electricity passed through it.

EDISON'S FILAMENT LIGHTBULB, 1879

hand in the home]

750 lb.: (340 kg)
the weight of the very first microwave oven, the Raytheon Radarange

1954
Color television
The United States became the first country with nationwide color TV broadcasts, and many electronics companies began selling color sets.

FAMILY VIEWING, 1950s

FERGUSON 306T TELEVISION, UK, 1956

1929
The first electric razor, invented by Colonel Jacob Schick, went on sale in the US.

1947
US company Raytheon produced the first microwave oven. It stood more than 6 feet (1.8 m) tall.

1955
In the US, Eugene Polley designed the first wireless TV remote control, the Zenith Flash-Matic.

2011
LG developed a smart fridge that connects to the Internet. Owners can check its contents by phone while out shopping.

•1930 •1940 •2000

1927
American J. W. Hammes built a garbage disposal system that ground up food waste so it could be flushed down a drain.

1956
French couple Marc and Colette Grégoire made the first nonstick pans, which were coated with a slippery material called Teflon.

2010
3-D TV sets, made by Panasonic, Samsung, and LG, became widely available in stores in the US and UK.

1922
Electric blender
Stephen Poplawski, a Polish-born American, invented the blender, which uses spinning blades to liquefy food. Many stores bought his machine to make drinks such as milk shakes.

EARLY ELECTRIC BLENDER

1983
Dyson vacuum
After five years of testing and more than 5,000 prototypes, British industrial designer James Dyson built the first cyclonic vacuum cleaner, the G-Force. Cyclonic vacuums use swirling air to capture dust and dirt. Previously, all vacuums contained bags to collect dust.

DYSON WITH HIS 2005 BALL VACUUM CLEANER

JAMES DYSON
British inventor
Founded: Dyson Ltd.
Invented: Cyclonic vacuum

Sports shoe [Get a grip!]

A modern athletic shoe is a triumph of engineering. Designed by computer, dozens of different materials are glued, stitched, or fitted together with precision.

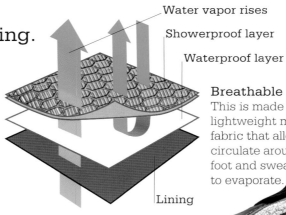

Water vapor rises

Showerproof layer

Waterproof layer

Lining

Laces
Laces are made of 40 or more individual cotton or polyester threads woven together by machine.

Breathable upper
This is made of a lightweight mesh fabric that allows air to circulate around the foot and sweat to evaporate.

Vintage soccer boot
This 1930s soccer boot made from thick leather got heavier when it became wet. Screwed-in studs made of plastic and rubber—for gripping the turf—were introduced in the 1950s.

Running shoe

A modern running shoe needs to protect and support a runner's foot yet still be lightweight. As many as 20 cutting-edge materials may make up a single shoe, radically reducing the weight. Some shoes weigh as little as 5–7 oz. (142–198 g) each.

Breathable upper

Toe bumper
Made of molded rubber or plastic, this adds protection to the front of the shoe and prevents stubbed toes.

Cushioned insole
This is cut out of sheets of polyurethane foam and often treated with chemicals to neutralize foot odor.

Midsole
Often made of molded plastic, this gives the shoe its shape and supports the arch of your foot.

Gel pad

Foot impact

The pad absorbs some impact.

Force spreads outward.

Gel pad
A pad of silicon gel helps absorb the shock when the ball of your foot strikes the ground.

Tongue
The foam for this is made by injecting millions of tiny air bubbles into a plastic liquid and letting it set.

Ankle support
Made of soft plastic foam to cushion your heel, this keeps you from slipping out of the shoe.

Reflective strips

Reflective strips
Tiny plastic prisms reflect 80 percent of light and make runners safely visible at night.

VIEW FROM ABOVE

Light out   Light in

SIDE VIEW

Heel cushion
This springy molded foam spreads the impact as your heel strikes the ground.

Hard-wearing tread
The rubber-based tread can grip wet, slippery surfaces.

Biomechanics
The study of how your body moves is called biomechanics. Footwear makers use it to help them design better sports shoes. Running is a repetitive set of movements, with several thousand steps taken for every hour of exercise.

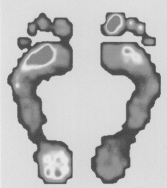

Impact pressure
Pressure sensors can measure the impact of your weight on the soles of your feet. This color-coded image shows different levels of pressure, with red areas having the most.

Recording data
High-speed cameras can capture the positions of athletes' feet, ankles, and legs as they leave the starting blocks and get into their running stride. These images are used to determine the forces and strains on the foot and the shoe.

$2.42
billion: the amount spent on running and jogging shoes in the US in 2010

Human engineering

Health technology already assists many people. They may use motorized wheelchairs, hearing aids, prostheses (artificial body parts), and artificial implants to replace failing or missing parts. In the future, technology may replace more and more of the human body.

Human upgrade

Some futuristic films feature cyborgs—beings that are part human and part machine, with technology that gives them abilities superior to ordinary people's. Although cyborgs are fictional, some artificial body parts being built today can match or even outperform their natural equivalents.

Film cyborg
In *The Terminator* (1984), a powerful cyborg is sent back in time from 2029.

Hand

i-limb ultra
High-tech artificial hands, such as the i-limb ultra, offer realistic movement. They use touch and force sensors to adjust the strength of their grip. The i-limb ultra can carry a load of up to 198.4 pounds (90 kg).

Skin

Made in the laboratory
New skin can be made by growing skin cells over a framework built of collagen, a protein found in body tissues. Scientists hope to be able to interweave artificial nerve fibers into the skin to give it the sense of touch.

Artificial skin grows over an ear-shaped structure.

Chip

Microchip implants
One day, a microchip under the skin may be able to send radio signals to confirm a person's identity or inform doctors of a patient's medical conditions. Some chips might even run GPS (see pages 30–31), enabling rescuers to find lost people.

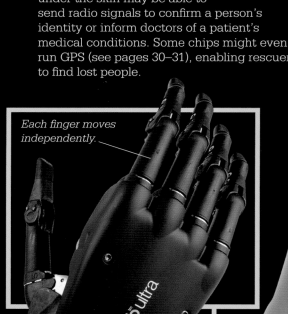

Each finger moves independently.

i-limb ultra
touch bionics

Eye

Argus II

This system restores some sight to blind or partially sighted people. It uses a camera mounted on eyeglasses to relay video signals to electrodes in an implant in the eye. The electrodes then send electrical signals to the brain via the optic nerve.

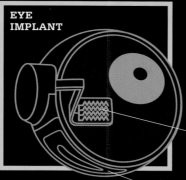

EYE IMPLANT

Tiny electrodes

An antenna communicates with the camera.

Flex-Foot

The Flex-Foot Cheetah is a carbon-fiber prosthetic lower leg and foot. It squashes and bends as it lands, then springs back into shape to drive the runner forward.

Spring power
South African sprinter Oscar Pistorius uses a Flex-Foot on each leg when he runs in races.

Opening for blood flow

Heart

AbioCor implant

The AbioCor, a complete replacement heart, pumps up to 2.5 gallons (12 L) of blood around the body per minute. It is powered by a battery pack worn on the hip and an implanted rechargeable battery.

AbioCor contains a motor-driven hydraulic pumping system.

Hip

Artificial ball-and-socket joint

The dishlike socket fits into the pelvis, and the ball joint attaches to the femur (thigh bone). Hip replacement operations often use a robot to drill accurately into the patient's femur so that the prosthetic can be fitted.

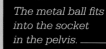

The metal ball fits into the socket in the pelvis.

The plastic body fits into the femur.

Nanorobots

Someday, doctors may be able to inject microscopic devices called nanorobots into the body. Once inside, nanorobots could clear blood vessels of fatty deposits, repair damaged tissues, monitor health, and release medicines.

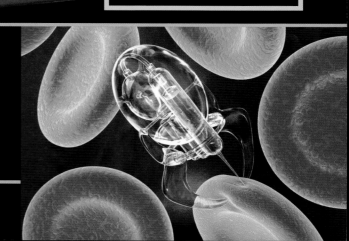

Faster than the wind

In 2009, in California, the Ecotricity Greenbird achieved a speed of 126.2 miles per hour (203.1 kph)—a world record for a wind-powered land vehicle. Built of carbon-fiber materials, the Greenbird is a land yacht. Unlike other land yachts, it uses a solid vertical wing instead of a cloth sail to harness the wind and propel itself forward over ice or dry lake beds.

Wind and waves [Power from

Using technology, we can harness the energy of rushing winds and crashing waves to generate electricity. Like solar power (see pages 102–103), these pollution-free energy sources will never run out.

Mills and pumps

The ancient Chinese and Babylonians first used windmills to grind wheat and other grains into flour more than 2,000 years ago. Other early wind-powered machines pumped water up from wells. Wind pumps are still used today on farms and in isolated places.

Greek windmill
Gears transmit the sails' turning motion to large, round grinding stones.

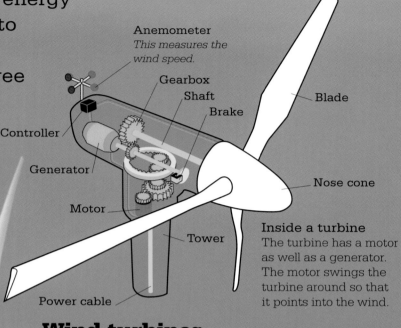

Anemometer
This measures the wind speed.

Gearbox
Shaft
Brake

Controller

Generator

Motor

Tower

Power cable

Blade

Nose cone

Inside a turbine
The turbine has a motor as well as a generator. The motor swings the turbine around so that it points into the wind.

Wind turbines

Horizontal-axis wind turbines have propeller-like blades. As the blades rotate in the wind, they spin a shaft that drives a generator. The electricity produced supplies factories, offices, and homes. Producing electricity from wind power avoids using up the world's limited supplies of fossil fuels (see page 90).

Offshore wind farm
Perched on top of tall towers at sea or on land, wind turbines grouped together in clusters are called wind farms.

5,000:
the number of homes
that can be powered by an ENERCON E-126 wind turbine

nature]

Types of turbine

A turbine's power depends on its location and size. Large horizontal-axis turbines, such as the huge ENERCON E-126, are the most powerful. Vertical-axis designs, such as helical, Darrieus, and Savonius turbines, are easier to build since they can be placed closer to the ground.

Horizontal-axis
This needs to point into the wind to work.

Helical-Darrieus
This works when wind gusts from all directions.

Darrieus
This spins when air catches its two blades.

Savonius
This is mounted on a rotating shaft.

Harnessing waves

In an oscillating water column system, such as the LIMPET on the Scottish island of Islay, the advance and retreat of ocean waves push air past a special set of blades called a Wells turbine. The rotation of the turbine drives a generator that produces electricity.

Islay LIMPET
This device produces enough electricity to power 400 homes.

1 Water in
As the waves break, water flows into a chamber. The water pushes air out, spinning the Wells turbine's blades.

Air out
The turbine spins as air is forced out.

2 Water out
When the water recedes, air is sucked into the chamber. The air flows over the turbine and spins its blades once again.

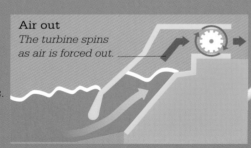

Air in
As it enters, air spins the turbine.

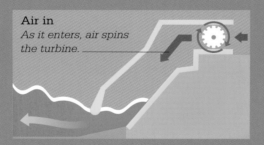

Solar power [Energy from

The Sun sends out huge amounts of energy. Some of it reaches Earth and warms the planet, letting life flourish here. The Sun's energy can also help generate power without burning fossil fuels (coal, oil, and natural gas) and creating pollution.

Cruising the ocean
The twin-hulled, 102-foot (31 m) *PlanetSolar* has a maximum speed of 16 mph (26 kph).

PlanetSolar
The top of this boat is covered with 5,780 sq. ft. (537 sq. m.) of photovoltaic panels, each one a collection of cells (see below). The electricity they produce powers motors that turn the boat's propellers.

Built by	Knierim Yacht Club, Kiel, Germany
Used for	Traveling around the world by solar-powered boat
Introduced	2010

Nieuwland roof tiles
Over 500 homes in Nieuwland, the Netherlands, have roofs made of photovoltaic panels rather than roof tiles. Together, they generate 1.35 million watts of power.

Built by	REMU and the city of Amersfoort, the Netherlands
Used for	Providing electricity to schools and homes
Introduced	1995

Rooftop providers
The roof panels supply enough power to meet most of each home's electricity needs.

Photovoltaic cell
In a photovoltaic (PV) cell, sunlight knocks negatively charged particles called electrons off atoms. The electrons then flow as an electric current.

Inside a PV cell
Two layers of semiconductor material are sandwiched between electrically charged plates.

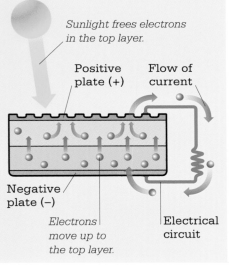

Sunlight frees electrons in the top layer.

Positive plate (+)

Flow of current

Negative plate (−)

Electrons move up to the top layer.

Electrical circuit

Converter pack
The small photovoltaic panels on the Converter Solar Backpack can be used to recharge a device stored inside, such as a cellular phone or an MP3 player. An hour of sunlight gives a phone enough power for two to three hours of talk time.

Built by	Voltaic Systems, US
Used for	Recharging the batteries of small electrical devices
Introduced	2004

Power pack
Each of the two PV panels provides 2 watts of power.

NLV Quant
The experimental Quant car has electric motors (see page 65) rather than a gas engine. The car is coated with a thin photovoltaic film, which converts sunlight into electricity to drive the motors.

Built by	NLV Solar AG, Switzerland
Used for	Driving with solar power at up to 234 mph (377 kph)
Introduced	2012

NLV QUANT

PHOTOVOLTAIC PYRITE FILM

Mineral coating
The film is made from the mineral pyrite, also known as fool's gold.

sunlight]

Odeillo furnace

Solar furnaces use mirrors to concentrate the energy of the Sun's rays onto a small area. The intense heat generated can be used to melt metals or turn water into steam for driving electricity generators.

Built by	National Center for Scientific Research, Odeillo, France
Used for	Testing metals and other materials; generating electricity
Introduced	1970

Mirrors focus the Sun's rays onto a crucible.

Extreme heat melts the solid ore inside the crucible.

Molten metal pours out into molds.

Metal from ore

Solar furnaces can produce metals from ores (rocks that contain metal) without using much electricity.

6,330 °F (3,500°C):

the maximum temperature reached at the Odeillo solar furnace

Reflecting dish

Odeillo uses 63 flat mirrors arranged in a dish shape to focus sunlight on the central tower containing the crucible.

Eco-city, day and night

Masdar City, in the United Arab Emirates, will be home to 50,000 people when it is completed in 2016. It will produce most of its energy at solar-power plants and recycle almost all of its waste. No gas-powered cars will be allowed in Masdar. Instead, people will walk or use pod cars—small vehicles that run on solar electricity. During the daytime (left), the main square will be shaded by giant parasols that capture energy from sunlight. At night (right), the parasols will fold up and release the energy as heat.

MASDAR CITY, UNITED ARAB EMIRATES

Acceleration
The increase in speed of an object.

Accelerometer
A sensor that detects and measures movement.

Aerodynamics
The study of how air passes over and around objects. Aerodynamics research can help vehicles such as aircraft and cars move through air more smoothly, to travel faster or use less fuel.

Airfoil
A wing-shaped device that generates the force of lift when it travels through air.

Altitude
The height above sea or ground level of an object in space or Earth's atmosphere.

Amplification
The increase in the loudness of a sound.

App
A computer program that performs a task, such as entering text or playing a sound file. *App* is short for *application*.

Artificial intelligence
The science and study of building machines with the ability to learn and think in humanlike ways.

Autonomous
Having the ability to make decisions and work alone without a human supervisor, as some robots can.

Bit
The smallest unit of computer memory that can be represented by an electrical signal as on or off. Eight bits make up a byte. *Bit* is short for *binary digit*.

Blog
An updatable web page used as a diary or journal, available for others to read on the World Wide Web. *Blog* is short for *web log*.

Bluetooth
A wireless communications system that uses radio waves to transmit data over short distances.

Bug
A hidden device, used by spies, that usually contains a microphone and a transmitter. Bugs secretly collect and transmit conversations and other sounds.

Catalytic converter
A device in a motor vehicle that removes some of the harmful polluting chemicals in the gases emitted by the vehicle's engine.

Circuit board
A sheet of insulating material on which components in electronic equipment are mounted.

Client
A computer or device that requests information in a computer network.

Combustion
The chemical reaction between a fuel and oxygen that produces heat and, usually, light.

Controller
The part of a robot that receives information from its sensors and makes decisions about how to control the rest of the robot.

CPU
A microprocessor that controls many of the functions of a computer. *CPU* stands for *central processing unit*.

Digital
Operating with data or information in numerical form. Modern computers use digital processing techniques.

Drag
The resistance that a vehicle or other moving object experiences when it travels through air. This force slows the object down.

Electromagnet
A form of magnet that can be switched on and off. When it is turned on, electricity flows through a coil of wire, creating a magnetic field.

End effector
A tool, such as a paint-spraying gun or gripping hand, that can be attached to a robot so that it is able to perform a task.

Exabyte (EB)
A unit of computer memory storage space that is equal to 1 quintillion bytes.

Gigabyte (GB)
A unit of computer memory storage space that is equal to 1,024 megabytes (MB).

GPS
A satellite system orbiting Earth and tells users their exact location and the correct time. *GPS* stands for *Global Positioning System*.

Gravity
The force that pulls objects together. Gravity causes objects to be pulled toward a planet.

Hybrid vehicle
A motor vehicle that has both an internal combustion engine and a rechargeable motor or energy system to reduce fuel use.

Hydraulic
Moved or operated by pressurized liquid in tubes.

Inclinometer
A sensor that measures the angles of slopes.

Internet
A global network that connects computers worldwide and allows them to communicate by sending information in small units.

Internet traffic
The amount of data sent via the Internet.

IT
The industry that is concerned with computing. *IT* stands for *information technology*.

More than 1 billion transistors are made every second

Glossary

Kilobyte (KB)
A unit of computer memory that is equal to 1,024 bytes.

LED
A small device that shines light when powered by electricity. *LED* stands for *light-emitting diode.*

Lenticular lens
A curved lens that allows each eye to see a different image of the same object at exactly the same time.

Lift
The force needed to raise an object such as a plane or spacecraft into the air and keep it from falling.

Light-year (ly)
A unit equal to the distance that light can travel in one year in empty space. A light-year is approximately 5.9 trillion miles (9.5 trillion km).

Megabyte (MB)
A unit of computer memory storage space that is equal to 1,024 kilobytes (KB).

Microchip
A collection of microscopic electronic circuits on a small piece of semiconductor material such as silicon.

Microphone
A device that converts sound waves into electrical signals that can be recorded or amplified.

Microprocessor
A computer processor consisting of microscopic electronic circuits and components contained on a single wafer of silicon.

Microsurgery
Internal surgery that uses tiny tools and cameras to give the surgeon a good view inside the body.

A NeXT computer used by Tim Berners-Lee was the world's first web server

Motherboard
The main circuit board in a personal computer, containing many of its key parts, including its central processing unit (CPU).

MTSO
A computer system that tracks phone calls and their locations, transfers calls between cells, and monitors the length and cost of calls. *MTSO* stands for *Mobile Telephone Switching Office.*

Nanotechnology
The science of building machines and robots in tiny sizes measured in nanometers. A nanometer is a billionth of a meter.

Network
A connection between two or more computers that enables them to communicate.

Operating system
A program or collection of programs that manages a computer or smartphone's resources and parts. Apple iOS, Windows 7, and Android are all common operating systems.

Particle accelerator
A machine that uses magnets to accelerate particles around a track. Collisions between the particles release huge amounts of energy and sometimes create new particles or new elements.

Photovoltaic cell
A small device, made of multiple layers, that produces electricity when light shines on its surface.

Pneumatic
Filled with air, or moved or operated by pressurized air in tubes.

Propeller
A set of blades that spin in air or water to make a vehicle move.

Prototype
An early model of a new product—usually full size and operational—that is designed for testing or publicity.

RAM
The memory space used by a computer to perform calculations and tasks or for storage of data. *RAM* stands for *random-access memory.*

Robotics
The branch of science and technology that develops machines that perform tasks automatically.

Rocket
A missile or vehicle that is propelled by the combustion of a fuel and a contained oxygen supply. A rocket ejects gases to thrust the vehicle forward or upward.

ROM
The memory space used by a computer to permanently store program instructions, operative procedures, or other data. *ROM* stands for *read-only memory.*

Rotor blade
A long, thin airfoil that spins to generate lift to support a helicopter in the air.

Satellite
An object that orbits a planet or another body. Satellites can be natural, such as the Moon, or made by people, such as communications satellites that relay TV pictures around Earth.

Search engine
A giant database of websites that can be searched and accessed by users on the Internet.

Semiconductor
A material whose electrical conductivity is between that of a metal and a nonmetal. Silicon is a semiconductive material used in many technologies.

Sensor
A device that can detect (and sometimes measure) aspects of its surroundings, such as heat, light, and movement.

Server
A computer that relays data or resources to client computers in a computer network.

SIM card
A small card with a microchip that holds cell phone data, such as phone numbers. *SIM* stands for *subscriber identity module.*

Simulator

A machine or computer program that models, or simulates, a real-life situation—such as flying an aircraft—for research or training.

SMS

A system that allows cell phones to send and receive text messages of up to 160 characters. *SMS* stands for *short message service.*

Software

Programs that instruct a computer how to operate and perform tasks.

Space probe

A scientific machine sent into space by rocket or shuttle to travel past or land on planets, moons, and other objects in space and investigate them.

Stereoscopic 3-D

A system that uses two images, one for each eye, to create a 3-D effect.

Suspension

A system of springs, shock absorbers, and other components directly connected to the wheels or axles of a vehicle that affects its handling.

Tablet

A type of computing device, such as the iPad or Galaxy Tab, that uses a flat touch-screen display.

Telescope

An instrument used to observe distant objects by collecting and focusing their electromagnetic radiation. Optical telescopes observe visible light, and radio telescopes detect radio waves.

Thrust

The force, usually generated by an engine, that pushes a vehicle forward.

Touch screen

An input device for computers or cell phones that displays options on a flat screen. Options are selected by touching the screen.

Transistor

A small electronic switch that replaced much larger and less reliable vacuum tubes in electric circuitry. Transistors have helped make smaller, more powerful electronic technology possible.

Velocity

The measurement of the speed of an object when it is moving in a particular direction.

Virtual world

A computer-generated simulation of a three-dimensional (3-D) environment. Users are able to experience and interact with images in a virtual world.

VTOL

The ability of some aircraft to rise straight up into the air without rolling along a runway to generate lift. *VTOL* stands for *vertical takeoff and landing.*

Website

A collection of pages or screens full of information that are made available to users over the World Wide Web.

Wi-Fi

A system that uses radio signals to allow computers and other devices to transmit and receive data over distances of up to a few hundred feet.

World Wide Web

The part of the Internet that contains a series of documents and resources linked together and viewed by a web browser.

APPLE iPAD TABLET

Index

PHOTOGRAPHY

1: Kulka/Corbis; 2–3: Maximilien Brice, CERN/Science Photo Library; 4cl: Science and Society/SuperStock; 6: Lockheed Martin Corporation; 7l: Kiyoshi Ota/X02055/Reuters/Corbis; 7cl: Bettmann/Corbis; 7cr: NASA; 7r: FLPA/Robin Chittenden/age fotostock; 8–9: Mona Lisa Production/Photo Researchers, Inc.; 10–11: NASA; 12c: B&C Alexander/Photo Researchers, Inc.; 12r: Kiyoshi Ota/X02055/Reuters/Corbis; 14tr: Ted Soqui/Corbis; 14bl: Nokia; 14bcl: Getty Images; 14bcr: Bloomberg via Getty Images; 14br: Science and Society/SuperStock; 15 (valve): Leif Norman/iStockphoto; 15 (transistor): Alexander Khromtsov/iStockphoto; 15 (microchip): alxpin/iStockphoto; 15bl: Science and Society/SuperStock; 15bc: Scott Aiken/Rex USA; 15br: LG; 16–17: Andrew Brookes/Corbis; 18–19 (MacBook Pro): Scholastic; 19tl: Rebelpilot/Flickr/Wikipedia; 19tc: iStockphoto; 20ct: iStockphoto; 23 (app icons): iStockphoto; 24tc: Science Source/Photo Researchers, Inc.; 24tr, 24b: Science Museum/Science & Society Picture Library; 25tl: Deborah Feingold/Corbis; 25tc: Peter Menzel/Photo Researchers, Inc.; 25tr: Mike Agliolo/Photo Researchers, Inc.; 25bl: Hank Morgan/Photo Researchers, Inc.; 25br: PSL Images/Alamy; 26–27 (Microsoft data center): Richard Duval/Microsoft; 26bl, 26br, 27bl: iStockphoto; 27br: Spanish Facebook; 30tl: Friedrich Saurer/Photo Researchers, Inc.; 30–31 (shark): iStockphoto; 31tr: Pixellover RM 10/Alamy; 31cr: Rafael Macia/Photo Researchers, Inc.; 31br: B&C Alexander/Photo Researchers, Inc.; 32–33 (Large Hadron Collider), 33bl: CERN; 33cr: Thierry Berrod, Mona Lisa Production/Photo Researchers, Inc.; 33br: Ali Yazdani & Daniel J. Hornbaker/Photo Researchers, Inc.; 34 (Goldfinger): AF archive/Alamy; 34cm: Wikipedia; 34cr: Corbis; 34br: Bettmann/Corbis; 35tl: SSPL via Getty Images; 35tr: Bettmann/Corbis; 35cl: Corbis; 35 (Gary Powers): Time & Life Pictures/Getty Images; 35 (memory stick): iStockphoto; 35 (Anna Chapman): Maxim Shipenkov/epa/Corbis; 35b: Getty Images; 36tl, 36 (arm tools), 36–37 (PackBot): iRobot; 37tr: AF archive/Alamy; 38–39: Kiyoshi Ota/X02055/Reuters/Corbis; 40tl: iStockphoto; 40tr: Science Source/Photo Researchers, Inc.; 40cl: John Zich/zrImages/Corbis; 40bl: David Vaughan/Photo Researchers, Inc.; 40br: Gostai, Inc.; 41: Sam Ogden/Photo Researchers, Inc.; 42l: AF archive/Alamy; 42c: Six Flags, Inc.; 44tl: Science and Society/SuperStock; 44tr: peter jordan/Alamy; 44bl: Science and Society/SuperStock; 44bc: Ralf-Finn Hestoft/Corbis; 44br: ArcadeImages/Alamy; 45tl: Haruyoshi Yamaguchi/Corbis; 45tr: Lightly Salted/Alamy; 45bl: Reuters/Corbis; 45bc: David Lee/Alamy; 45br: Oliver Berg/dpa/Corbis; 46tl, 46tr, 46 (Angry Birds on tablet), 46 (Angry Birds on phone): iStockphoto; 46cm: Bandai Namco Games; 46cr: Nintendo; 47tl: Lightly Salted/Alamy; 47tc: iStockphoto; 47tr: iControlPad; 47cl: Nintendo; 47cm: Microsoft Xbox; 47cr: iControlPad; 48tl: iStockphoto; 50–51 (CAVE): Teesside University; 52–53 (audience): Bettmann/Corbis; 53cr: AF archive/Alamy; 53br: Pascal Goetgheluck/Photo Researchers, Inc.; 54l, 55br: iStockphoto; 56tl: Tim Mosenfelder/Corbis; 58tl: Gamma-Rapho via Getty Images; 58tr: Getty Images; 58c: Robert Cianflone/Getty Images; 58bl: Six Flags Great Adventure/Splash/Newscom; 58br: Ahmad Yusni/epa/Corbis; 59: Sinibomb Images/Alamy; 59b: travelibUK/Alamy; 60–61: Six Flags, Inc.; 62l: AFP/Getty Images; 62c: NASA; 62tr: Keith Kent/Science Photo Library; 64–65 (Boeing): Grégoire Delatte; 66tl: Carnundrum/Alamy; 67cr: Transtock/SuperStock; 68tl: Motoring Picture Library/Alamy; 68tr: John Cairns/Alamy; 68bl: Omikron/Photo Researchers, Inc.; 68br: David Woods/Corbis; 69tl: PhotoStock10/Shutterstock; 69tr: Getty Images; 69bl: Microvision; 69br: izmostock/Alamy; 70tl: NASA Archive/Alamy; 70tr: ZUMA Press/Newscom; 70c: Edwards Air Force Base; 70bl: Tony Watson/Alamy; 70br: A kal fj/APimages; 71: Eric Risberg/APimages; 71br: Richard Meredith Hardy/RexUSA; 72–73: f1h2o, inc; 74cl: Tristar Photos/Alamy; 74bl: Simon Price/Alamy; 75: Richard Cooke/Alamy; 75br: NASA Ames Research Center/Photo Researchers, Inc.; 76–77 (WaveRunner): Gerald Julien/Getty Images; 77tl: Skyscan/Photo Researchers, Inc.; 77br: National Geographic Image Collection/Alamy; 78–79 (Endeavour): NASA; 79 (Saturn V): Friedrich Saurer/Photo Researchers, Inc.; 79 (Long March): China Great Wall Industry Corporation/Photo Researchers, Inc.; 79 (space shuttle): Photo Researchers, Inc.; 79 (Ariane 5): Reuters/Corbis; 79 (Soyuz-FG): NASA/Photo Researchers, Inc.; 80–81 (all), 82–83 (International Space Station), 83cr, 83br: NASA; 84l: Photo Researchers, Inc.; 84c: Science and Society/SuperStock; 86tl: SuperStock/Getty Images; 86bl, 87tr, 87br: iStockphoto; 88–89: Joe Fox/Alamy; 92tl: Nik Wheeler/Corbis; 92tr: Science and Society/SuperStock; 92bl: SSPL via Getty Images; 92br: Science and Society/SuperStock; 93tl: David Wooley/Getty Images; 93tr: Science and Society/SuperStock; 93bl: Comstock/Getty Images; 93br: Getty Images; 94tl: iStockphoto; 95tr: Alfred Pasieka/Photo Researchers, Inc.; 95br: Gustoimages/Photo Researchers, Inc.; 96tr: Shawn Hempel/Shutterstock; 96cl: Photos 12/Alamy; 96cr: James King-Holmes/Photo Researchers, Inc.; 96br: i-limb ultra; 96–97 (body): Science Picture Company; 97cl: Abiomed; 97 (Flex-Foot): Össur; 97 (Oscar Pistorius): Eric Lalmand/epa/Corbis; 97 (hip joint): Alexander Tsiaras/Photo Researchers, Inc.; 97br: Coneyl Jay/Photo Researchers, Inc.; 98–99: Greenbird, Inc.; 100–101 (wind farm): FLPA/Robin Chittenden/age fotostock; 100tl: Sunpix Travel/Alamy; 101tl: iStockphoto; 101tcl: Martin Bond/Photo Researchers, Inc.; 101tcr: Tom McHugh/Photo Researchers, Inc.; 101tr: Helix Wind; 101c: Martin Bond/Photo Researchers, Inc.; 102tl: Planet Solar SA, Inc.; 102tr: Clynt Garnham Renewable Energy/Alamy; 102cr: Voltaic, Inc.; 102bl, 102br: Quant, Inc.; 103b: Photo Researchers, Inc.; 104–105: LAVA (Laboratory for Visionary Architecture); 104br: Fosters & Partners, London; 108: Hugh Threlfall/Alamy.

ARTWORK

12l, 20–21 (smartphone), 42r, 48–49 (camcorder), 56–57 (guitar), 66–67 (car), 84r, 86–87 (bike), 94–95 (shoe): Tim Loughhead/Precision Illustration; all other artwork: Scholastic.

COVER

Front cover: (tablet surrounding icons) Hbas/Shutterstock; (icons) Lana Rinck/Shutterstock and iStockphoto; (finger) Discpicture/Shutterstock. Back cover: (robot hand) iStockphoto; (handheld electronic game) Kevork Djansezian/Getty Images; (computer screen) Manaemedia/Dreamstime.

Credits and acknowledgments